The Best Pathfinder Walks

COMPILED BY BRIAN CONDUIT

While every care has been taken to ensure the accuracy of
the route directions, the publishers cannot accept responsibility
for errors or omissions, or for changes in details given. It has
to be emphasised that the countryside is not static: hedges and
fences can be removed, field boundaries can alter, footpaths
can be rerouted and changes of ownership can result in the
closure or diversion of some concessionary paths. Also paths
that are easy and pleasant for walking in fine conditions may
become slippery, muddy and difficult in wet weather and
stepping-stones over rivers and streams may become impassable.
If readers know of any changes which have taken place Jarrold
Publishing would be grateful to hear from them.

First published 1994 by Ordnance Survey and Jarrold Publishing

Ordnance Survey   Jarrold Publishing
Romsey Road   Whitefriars
Maybush   Norwich NR3 1TR
Southampton SO16 4GU

Ordnance Survey ISBN 0-319-00494-5
Jarrold Publishing ISBN 0-7117-0813-4

Printed in Belgium

Contents

Introduction

Walking in the countryside is one of the most popular leisure and recreational pastimes in Britain. It is also one of the cheapest, involving less initial capital outlay than almost any other form of activity. The benefits that it brings to its devotees are many and varied: fresh air and exercise, physical and mental well-being, relaxation, escape from the pressures of everyday life, appreciation of natural beauty, and for those who join a club or walk with companions, comradeship.

An essential item is a map, and the most detailed maps for walkers are the Ordnance Survey Pathfinder and Outdoor Leisure maps. In theory with one of these every walker ought to be able to work out a route and do it without running into any difficulties. However despite substantial improvements to the footpath network over the last decade walkers can still encounter the familiar problems of poor waymarking, broken-down stiles, non-existent footbridges, locked gates and various illegal obstructions and diversions on rights of way. Even where such problems do not exist, new or inexperienced walkers may be hesitant about following a route across fields where the right of way legally exists and is clearly shown on the map but is not actually visible on the ground, a common occurrence.

One solution to these problems is to find a suitable walking guide to the area in which you are interested and choose routes from that. The Pathfinder series of guides, based on Ordnance Survey's Pathfinder and Outdoor Leisure maps, was created to provide collections of walks spread over a well-defined area, of varying lengths and degrees of difficulty, well researched and with detailed route instructions. The series now covers most of England and Wales and large parts of Scotland, and is still growing. In each title the twenty-eight walks try to cover the different types of terrain found in the region, include major places of interest and take in the most outstanding viewpoints. They range from short and easy strolls of about a couple of hours or so to more energetic half-day walks, with a few longer and more demanding day hikes. The aim is to cater for all types of walkers and their interests with perhaps a concentration on the less experienced who may not be skilled in map reading and navigation but who want to enjoy an interesting and trouble-free walk in attractive countryside with friends or family – a walk that is not too long or strenuous and leaves enough time to pop into a pub, tearoom or café either at the end or en route. Some might say that is the recipe for the perfect day, especially if blessed with the bonus of fine weather.

Earlier titles in the series concentrated on the national parks and other obvious walking areas and more recent ones include some less well-known and less-frequented areas that still have great scope for satisfying and interesting walks. With the more popular areas becoming very crowded and faced with ever-growing problems of footpath erosion, it is highly desirable that the less well-known areas attract more walkers. Not only does this give the over-used paths chance to recover but under-used paths are likely to remain open and become less overgrown and difficult to walk. The Pathfinder series tries to be as easy to use as possible, providing clear route directions, colour photographs, extracts from the relevant Ordnance Survey maps marked with the line of route, and information about parking and available refreshments.

This magnificent Lake District scenery includes the landmark of the Langdale Pikes

The walks are also colour coded according to the level of difficulty.

Now the series has enough titles to cover much of Britain, it seems appropriate to bring out a collection of some of the best of the Pathfinder walks, illustrating the rich variety of landscape, magnificent scenery and wide range of walking opportunities available. The choice has not been easy, and as with all such selections it is inevitably subjective. The aim has been to choose those walks which as far as possible combine fine scenery with some notable features of interest and group them under eight themes that illustrate the different aspects of walking in Britain. The themes cover riverside walks, walks in woodlands and forests, lowland walks, moorland and downland walks, coastal walks, walks in hills and mountains, and walks that have a particular heritage flavour. The final section, of four 'walks on the wild side', has walks that venture into wilderness areas and are recommended only for those who are fit and have experience in walking in such areas and the ability to navigate by using a compass. Variety is one of the main criteria for choosing Pathfinder walks, so those selected illustrate much more than the theme under which they are grouped.

Pathfinder guides are essentially practical guides, designed to take on walks, slipping easily into pocket or rucksack. In contrast this is an armchair walking book, with large photographs displaying Britain's magnificent scenery, to be read and enjoyed in comfort at home. Armchair walking may seem something of a contradiction but it is a most pleasurable occupation, especially on dark and dismal winter evenings. It offers the opportunity to look both forwards and backwards, reminiscing over past walks satisfactorily accomplished and looking forward to and planning new walks for when the days become longer and you can venture forth again. Many might also enjoy the thrill of experiencing something of the flavour of some of these walks, especially the more strenuous and challenging ones, without necessarily wishing to experience them in reality.

Three major conclusions can be drawn from this collection of best walks, and indeed from the whole Pathfinder range. The first is that we are fortunate to be endowed with such a wide range of landscape and natural beauty within a comparatively small geographical area. Few countries can match the variety of the rugged, magnificent western Highlands of Scotland and the lonely coastal marshes of East Anglia, the gentle valleys and honey-coloured stone villages of the Cotswolds and the open moorland expanses of North Yorkshire, the long, smooth, grassy ridges of the Black Mountains in South Wales and the low, wooded slopes of Warwickshire's 'Shakespeare Country', and the chalk downs of Sussex and the heathery coastal moorlands of Exmoor.

A second conclusion is that regardless of where you live, attractive and unspoiled countryside lies near at hand and does not necessarily mean a lot of long-distance travelling. Even in heavily populated, industrialised areas it is surprising how quickly you can escape into rural surroundings. The final conclusion is that walking is an activity that is accessible to all. Whatever your age, stamina and level of fitness, there are walks here that can be enjoyed – whether they are short and easy strolls of a few miles in flat country, or long and strenuous ascents over rough terrain to some of the highest summits in the land.

It is hoped that this book serves not only to stimulate your imagination but also to whet your appetite so that as you read the descriptions of the walks, look at the maps and admire the pictures you will feel inspired to put on a pair of boots, grab a rucksack and appropriate clothing and go out into our beautiful and varied countryside.

Hadrian's Wall, the most northerly frontier of the Roman Empire, snakes across the wild, open Northumberland countryside, providing an excellent route for walkers

National parks and countryside recreation

Ten national parks were created in England and Wales as a result of an Act of Parliament in 1949, and an eleventh area was given the same protection under special legislation in 1989. In addition to these there are numerous specially designated areas of outstanding natural beauty, country and regional parks, sites of special scientific interest and picnic areas scattered throughout England, Wales and Scotland, all of which share the twin aims of preservation of the countryside and public accessibility and enjoyment.

In trying to define a national park, one point to bear in mind is that unlike many overseas ones Britain's national parks are not owned by the nation. The vast bulk of the land in them is under private ownership. John Dower, whose report in 1945 created their framework, defined a national park as 'an extensive area of beautiful and relatively wild country in which, for the nation's benefit and by appropriate national decision and action, (a) the characteristic landscape beauty is strictly preserved, (b) access and facilities for public open-air enjoyment are amply provided, (c) wildlife and buildings and places of architectural and historic interest are suitably protected, while (d) established farming use is effectively maintained'.

The concept of having designated areas of protected countryside grew out of a number of factors that appeared towards the end of the nineteenth century, principally greater facilities and opportunities for travel, the development of conservationist bodies and the establishment of national parks abroad. Apart from a few of the early individual travellers such as Celia Fiennes and Daniel Defoe – who were usually more concerned with commenting on agricultural improvements, the appearance of towns and the extent of antiquities to be found than with the wonders of nature – interest in the countryside as a source of beauty, spiritual refreshment and recreation, and along with that an interest in conserving it, did not arise until the Victorian era.

Towards the end of the eighteenth century improvements in road transport enabled the wealthy to visit regions that had hitherto been largely inaccessible; by the middle of the nineteenth century the construction of the railways opened up such possibilities to the middle classes and later on to the working classes in even greater numbers. At the same time the Romantic movement was in full swing, and encouraged by the works of Wordsworth, Coleridge and Shelley interest and enthusiasm for wild places, including the mountain, moorland and hill regions of northern and western Britain, were now in vogue. Eighteenth-century taste had thought of the Scottish Highlands,

Surprise View is a superb viewpoint above the eastern side of Derwentwater in the Lake District, the largest of Britain's national parks

the Lake District and Snowdonia as places to avoid, preferring controlled order and symmetry in nature as well as in architecture and town planning. But the upper- and middle-class Victorian travellers were thrilled and awed by what they saw as the untamed savagery and wilderness of mountain peaks, deep and secluded gorges, thundering waterfalls, towering cliffs and rocky crags. In addition there was a growing reaction against the materialism and squalor of Victorian industrialisation and urbanisation and a desire to escape from the formality and artificiality of town life into areas of unspoilt natural beauty.

A result of this was the formation of a number of different societies, all concerned with the 'great outdoors': naturalist groups, rambling clubs and conservationist organisations. One of the earliest of these was the Commons, Open Spaces and Footpaths Preservation Society, originally founded in 1865 to preserve commons and develop public access to the countryside. Particularly influential was the National Trust, set up in 1895 to protect and maintain both places of natural beauty and places of historic interest, and later on the Councils for the Preservation of Rural England, Wales and Scotland, three separate bodies, came into being between 1926 and 1928.

The world's first national park was the Yellowstone Park in the United States, designated in 1872. This was followed by others in Canada, South Africa, Germany, Switzerland, New Zealand and elsewhere, but in Britain such places did not come about until after the Second World War. Proposals for the creation of areas of protected countryside were made before the First World War and during the 1920s and 1930s, but nothing was done. The growing demand from people in towns for access to open country and the reluctance of landowners – particularly those who owned large expanses of uncultivated moorland – to grant it led to a number of ugly incidents, in particular the mass trespass in the Peak District in 1932, when fighting took place between ramblers and gamekeepers and some of the trespassers received stiff prison sentences.

It was in the climate exemplified by the Beveridge Report and the subsequent creation of the welfare state, however, that calls for countryside conservation and access came to fruition in parliament. Based on the recommendations of the Dower Report (1945) and the Hobhouse Committee (1947), the National Parks and Countryside Act of 1949 provided for the designation and preservation of areas both of great scenic beauty and of particular wildlife and scientific interest throughout Britain. More specifically it provided for the creation of national parks in England and Wales. Scotland was excluded because, as it had greater areas of open space and a smaller population, there were fewer pressures on the Scottish countryside and therefore there was felt to be less need for the creation of such protected areas.

A National Parks Commission was set up, and over the next eight years ten areas were designated as parks: seven in England (Northumberland, Lake District, North York Moors, Yorkshire Dales, Peak District, Exmoor and Dartmoor) and three in Wales (Snowdonia, Brecon Beacons and Pembrokeshire Coast). At the same time the commission was also given the responsibility for designating other smaller areas of high recreational and scenic qualities (areas of outstanding natural beauty), and the power to propose and develop long-distance footpaths, now called national trails, though it was not until 1965 that the first of these, the Pennine Way, came into existence.

Further changes came with the Countryside Act of 1968 (a similar one for Scotland had been passed in 1967). The National Parks Commission was replaced by the Countryside Commission, which was now to oversee and review virtually all aspects of countryside conservation, access and provision of recreational amenities. The country parks, which were smaller areas of countryside often close to urban areas, came into being. A number of long-distance footpaths were created, followed by an even greater number of unofficial long- or middle-distance paths, devised by individuals, ramblers' groups or local authorities. Provision of car parks and visitor centres, waymarking of public rights of way and the production of leaflets giving suggestions for walking routes all increased, a reflection of both increased leisure and a greater desire for recreational activity, of which walking in particular, now recognised as the most popular leisure pursuit, has had a great explosion of interest.

In 1989 the Norfolk and Suffolk Broads joined the national park family, special legislation covering the area's navigational interests as well as aspects of conservation and public enjoyment.

The authorities who administer the individual national parks have the very difficult task of reconciling the interests of the people who live and earn their living within them with those of the visitors. National parks, and the other designated areas, are not living museums. Developments of various kinds, in housing, transport and rural industries, are needed. There is pressure to exploit the resources of the area, through more intensive farming, or through increased quarrying and forestry, extraction of minerals or the construction of reservoirs.

In the end it all comes down to a question of balance – a balance between conservation and 'sensitive development'. On the one hand there is a responsibility to preserve and enhance the natural beauty of the national parks and to promote their enjoyment by the public, and on the other, the needs and well-being of the people living and working in them have to be borne in mind.

Marloes Sands is one of the finest beaches in the Pembrokeshire Coast National Park

The National Trust

Anyone who likes visiting places of natural beauty or historic interest has cause to be grateful to the National Trust. Without it many such places would probably have vanished by now, either under an avalanche of concrete and bricks and mortar or through reservoir construction or blanket afforestation.

It was in response to the pressures on the countryside posed by the relentless march of Victorian industrialisation that the trust was set up in 1895. Its founders, inspired by the common goals of protecting and conserving Britain's national heritage and widening public access to it, were Sir Robert Hunter, Octavia Hill and Canon Rawnsley, respectively a solicitor, a social reformer and a clergyman. The latter was particularly influential. As a canon of Carlisle Cathedral and vicar of Crosthwaite (near Keswick), he was concerned about threats to the Lake District and had already been active in protecting footpaths and promoting public access to open countryside. After the flooding of Thirlmere in 1879 to create a large reservoir, he and his two colleagues became increasingly convinced that the only effective protection was outright ownership of land.

The purpose of the National Trust is to preserve areas of natural beauty and sites of historic interest by acquisition, holding them in trust for the nation and making

The Seven Sisters, East Sussex. Many fine areas like this have National Trust protection

them available for public access and enjoyment. Some of its properties have been acquired through purchase, but many have been donated. Nowadays it is not only one of the biggest landowners in the country, but also one of the most active conservation charities, protecting well over half a million acres (200,000 ha) of land, including over 500 miles (800 km) of coastline and a large number of historic properties (houses, castles and gardens) in England, Wales and Northern Ireland. (There is a separate National Trust for Scotland, which was set up in 1931.)

Furthermore, once a piece of land has come under National Trust ownership, it is difficult for its status to be altered. As a result of parliamentary legislation in 1907, the trust was given the right to declare its property inalienable, so ensuring that in any dispute it can appeal directly to parliament.

As it works towards its dual aims of conserving areas of attractive countryside and encouraging greater public access (not easy to reconcile in this age of mass tourism), the trust provides an excellent service to walkers by creating new concessionary paths and waymarked trails, by maintaining stiles and footbridges and by combating the ever-increasing problem of footpath erosion.

The Ramblers' Association

No organisation works more actively to protect and extend the rights and interests of walkers in the countryside than the Ramblers' Association. Its aims (summarised here) are clear: to foster a greater knowledge, love and care of the countryside; to assist in the protection and enhancement of public rights of way and areas of natural beauty; to work for greater public access to the countryside; and to encourage more people to take up rambling as a healthy, recreational activity.

It was founded in 1935 when, following the setting up of a National Council of Ramblers' Federation in 1931, a number of federations earlier formed in London, Manchester, the Midlands and elsewhere came together to create a more effective pressure group to deal with such contemporary problems as the disappearance and obstruction of footpaths, the prevention of access to open mountain and moorland

and increasing hostility from landowners. This was the era of the mass trespasses, when there were sometimes violent confrontations between ramblers and gamekeepers, especially on the moorlands of the Peak District.

Since then the Ramblers' Association has played an influential role in preserving and developing the national footpath network, supporting the creation of national parks and encouraging the designation and waymarking of long-distance footpaths.

Our freedom to walk in the countryside is precarious, and requires constant vigilance. As well as the perennial problems of footpaths being illegally obstructed, disappearing through lack of use or extinguished by housing or road construction, new dangers can spring up at any time. It is to meet such problems and dangers that the Ramblers' Association exists and represents the interests of all walkers.

Walkers and the law

The average walker in a national park or other popular walking area, armed with the appropriate Ordnance Survey map, reinforced perhaps by a guidebook giving detailed walking instructions, is unlikely to run into legal difficulties, but it is useful to know something about the law relating to public rights of way. The right to walk over certain parts of the countryside has developed over a long period of time, and how such rights came into being and how far they are protected by the law is a complex subject, fascinating in its own right, but too lengthy to be discussed here. The following comments are intended simply to be a helpful guide, backed up by the Countryside Access Charter, a concise summary of walkers' rights and obligations drawn up by the Countryside Commission.

Basically there are two main kinds of public rights of way: footpaths (for walkers only) and bridleways (for walkers, riders on horseback and pedal cyclists). Footpaths and bridleways are shown by broken green lines on Ordnance Survey Pathfinder and Outdoor Leisure maps and broken red lines on Landranger maps. There is also a third category, called byways or 'roads used as a public path': chiefly broad, walled tracks (green lanes) or farm roads, which walkers, riders and cyclists have to share, usually only occasionally, with motor vehicles. Many of these public paths have been in existence for hundreds of years and some even originated as prehistoric trackways and have been in constant use for well over 2,000 years.

The term 'right of way' means exactly what it says. It gives right of passage over what, in the vast majority of cases, is private land, and you are required to keep to the line of the path and not stray onto the land either side. If you inadvertently wander off the right of way – either because of faulty map-reading or because the route is not clearly indicated on the ground – you are technically trespassing and the wisest course is to ask the nearest available person (farmer or fellow walker) to direct you

Walkers on the Chiltern escarpment enjoy this fine view looking towards Ivinghoe Beacon

back to the correct route. There are stories of unpleasant confrontations between walkers and farmers at times, but in general most farmers are helpful and co-operative when responding to a genuine and polite request for assistance in route finding.

Obstructions can sometimes be a problem and probably the most common of these is where a path across a field has been ploughed up. It is legal for a farmer to plough up a path provided that he restores it within two weeks, barring exceptionally bad

COUNTRYSIDE ACCESS CHARTER

Your rights of way are:

- *public footpaths – on foot only. Sometimes waymarked in yellow*
- *bridleways – on foot, horseback and pedal cycle. Sometimes waymarked in blue*
- *byways (usually old roads), most 'roads used as public paths' and, of course, public roads – all traffic has the right of way*

Use maps, signs and waymarks to check rights of way. Ordnance Survey Pathfinder and Landranger maps show most public rights of way.

On rights of way you can:

- *take a pram, pushchair or wheelchair if practicable*
- *take a dog (on a lead or under close control)*
- *take a short route round an illegal obstruction or remove it sufficiently to get past*

You have a right to go for recreation to:

- *public parks and open spaces – on foot*
- *most commons near older towns and cities – on foot and sometimes on horseback*
- *private land where the owner has a formal agreement with the local authority*

In addition you can use the following by local or established custom or consent, but ask for advice if you are unsure:

- *many areas of open country, such as moorland, fell and coastal areas, especially those in the care of the National Trust, and some commons*
- *some woods and forests, especially those owned by the Forestry Commission*
- *country parks and picnic sites*
- *most beaches*
- *canal towpaths*
- *some private paths and tracks*

Consent sometimes extends to horse-riding and cycling.

For your information:

- *county councils and London boroughs maintain and record rights of way, and register commons*
- *obstructions, dangerous animals, harassment and misleading signs on rights of way are illegal and you should report them to the county council*
- *paths across fields can be ploughed, but must normally be reinstated within two weeks*
- *landowners can require you to leave land to which you have no right of access*
- *motor vehicles are normally permitted only on roads, byways and some 'roads used as public paths'*

The seventeenth-century Essex Bridge over the River Trent was built to give access to Cannock Chase

By custom, though not by right, you are generally free to walk across the open and uncultivated higher land of mountain, moorland and fell, but this varies from area to area and from one season to another. Grouse moors, for example, will be out of bounds during the breeding and shooting seasons and some open areas are used as Ministry of Defence firing ranges, for which reason access will be restricted. In some areas the situation has been clarified as a result of 'access agreements' between the landowners and either the county council or the national park authority, which clearly define when and where you can walk over such open country.

In Scotland there are differences from the situation in the rest of Britain. Rights of way are not marked on Ordnance Survey maps, although local planning authorities have a duty to protect and maintain them. In the Highlands nearly every major glen or lochside will be a right of way, and it was not felt necessary to show these as such on the maps, a reflection

weather. This does not always happen and here the walker is presented with a dilemma: to follow the line of the path, even if this inevitably means treading on crops, or to use common sense and walk around the edge of the field. The latter course of action often seems the best, but as this means that you would be trespassing you are, in law, supposed to keep to the exact line of the path, avoiding unnecessary damage to crops. In the case of other obstructions which may block a path (illegal fences and locked gates etc.), common sense again has to be used in order to negotiate them by the easiest method (detour or removal). If you have any problems negotiating rights of way, you should report the matter to the rights of way department of the relevant county, borough or metropolitan district council. They will then take action with the landowner concerned.

Apart from rights of way enshrined by law there are a number of other paths available to walkers. Permissive or concessionary paths have been created where a landowner has given permission for the public to use a particular route across his land. The main problem with these is that as they have been granted as a concession, there is no legal right to use them and therefore they can be extinguished at any time. In practice many of these concessionary routes have been established on land owned either by large public bodies such as the Forestry Commission, or by a private one such as the National Trust, and as these mainly encourage walkers to use their paths they are unlikely to be closed unless a change of ownership occurs.

Walkers also have free access to country parks (except where requested to keep away from certain areas for ecological reasons, such as wildlife protection, woodland regeneration and safeguarding of rare plants), canal towpaths and most beaches.

of the greater freedom to roam that is enjoyed in Scotland. But a path on a map is no indication of a right of way, and many paths and tracks of great use to walkers were built by estates as stalking-paths or for private access. While you may traverse such paths taking due care to avoid damage to property and the natural environment, you should obey restricted access notices and if asked to leave do so.

The watchdog on rights of way in Scotland is the Scottish Rights of Way Society, based in Edinburgh, which produces a booklet on the Scottish legal position. Its green signposts, indicating the lines of historic routes, are a familiar sight by many Highland roads.

FOLLOW THE COUNTRY CODE
Enjoy the countryside and respect its life and work

- *Guard against all risk of fire*
- *Fasten all gates*
- *Keep your dogs under close control*
- *Keep to public paths across farmland*
- *Leave livestock, crops and machinery alone*
- *Use gates and stiles to cross fences, hedges and walls*

- *Take your litter home*
- *Help to keep all water clean*
- *Protect wildlife, plants and trees*
- *Take special care on country roads*
- *Make no unnecessary noise*

Reproduced by permission of the Countryside Commission

Walking safety

Walking in gentle and low-lying countryside has no real dangers but it is still sensible to take the same precautions as in more hilly terrain.

The most difficult hazard likely to be encountered in low-lying areas is mud, especially when walking along woodland and field paths, farm tracks and bridleways, and in summer an additional difficulty may be narrow and overgrown paths, particularly along the edges of cultivated fields. Neither should constitute a major problem provided that the appropriate footwear is worn.

Although the hills, mountains and moorlands of Britain are of modest height compared with those in many other countries, they need to be treated with respect. Friendly and inviting in good weather, they can quickly be transformed into wet, misty, windswept and potentially dangerous areas of wilderness in bad weather. Even on an outwardly fine and settled summer day, conditions can rapidly deteriorate at high altitudes, and in winter even more so.

It is therefore advisable to always take both warm and waterproof clothing, sufficient nourishing food, a hot drink, first-aid kit, torch and whistle. Wear suitable footwear, i.e. strong walking boots or shoes that give a good grip over rocky terrain and on slippery slopes. Try to obtain a local weather forecast and bear it in mind before you start. Do not be afraid to abandon your proposed route and return to your starting point in the event of a sudden and unexpected deterioration in the weather. Do not go alone and allow enough time to finish the walk well before nightfall.

A few walks venture into remote wilderness areas and others climb high summits. These are suitable only for fit and experienced hill walkers able to use a compass and should definitely not be tackled by anyone else during the winter months or in bad weather, especially high winds and mist.

MOUNTAIN RESCUE

In case of emergency the standard procedure is to dial 999 and ask for the police who will assess and deal with the situation.

First, however, render first aid as required and make sure the casualty is made warm and comfortable. The distress signal (six flashes/whistle-blasts, repeated at minute intervals) may bring help from other walkers in the area. Write down essential details: exact location (six-figure reference), time of accident, numbers involved, details of injuries, steps already taken; then despatch a messenger to phone the police.

If leaving the casualty alone mark the site with an eye-catching object. Be patient; waiting for help can seem interminable.

RIGHT *Take care in wild countryside like this in the Brecon Beacons*

Key for Ordnance Survey maps

ROADS AND PATHS
Not necessarily rights of way

M1 or A6(M)	M1 or A6(M)	Motorway
A 31(T)	A 31(T)	Trunk or Main road
B 3074	B 3074	Secondary road
A 35	A 35	Dual carriageway

Road generally more than 4m wide

Road generally less than 4m wide

Other road, drive or track

Unfenced roads and tracks are shown by pecked lines

.... Path

PUBLIC RIGHTS OF WAY
Public rights of way may not be evident on the ground

} Public paths { Footpath / Bridleway

++++++ Byway open to all traffic
+–+–+–+ Road used as a public path

DANGER AREA
Firing and test ranges in the area
Danger!
Observe warning notices

The indication of a towpath in this book does not necessarily imply a public right of way
The representation of any other road, track or path is no evidence of the existence of a right of way
Public rights of way are not shown on Ordnance Survey maps of Scotland

BOUNDARIES

— · — · — County (England and Wales)
Region or Islands Area (Scotland)

— — — — District

—•—•—•— London Borough

················· Civil Parish (England)* Community (Wales)

— — — — — Constituency (County, Borough, Burgh or European Assembly)

Coincident boundaries are shown by the first appropriate symbol

*For Ordnance Survey purposes County Boundary is deemed to be the limit of the parish structure whether or not a parish area adjoins

RAILWAYS

Multiple track ⎫ Standard
Single track ⎬ gauge
Narrow gauge ⎭
Siding
Cutting
Embankment
Tunnel
Road over; road under
Level crossing; station

VEGETATION
Limits of vegetation are defined by positioning of the symbols but may be delineated also by pecks or dots

Coniferous trees
Non-coniferous trees
Coppice

Orchard
Scrub
Marsh, reeds, saltings.

Bracken, rough grassland
In some areas bracken ( ) and rough grassland ( ) are shown separately
Heath

Shown collectively as rough grassland on some sheets

In some areas reeds ( ) and saltings ( ) are shown separately

HEIGHTS AND ROCK FEATURES

50 ·
285 } Determined by { ground survey / air survey

Surface heights are to the nearest metre above mean sea level. Heights shown close to a triangulation pillar refer to the ground level height at the pillar and not necessarily at the summit

Vertical face

Loose rock | Boulders | Outcrop | Scree

75
60 Contours are at
50 5 metres
vertical interval

TOURIST INFORMATION

† Abbey, Cathedral, Priory
🐟 Aquarium
⛺ Camp site
🚐 Caravan site
🏰 Castle
Cave
Country park
Craft centre
P Parking
PC Public Convenience (in rural areas)

𝔐 Ancient Monuments and Historic Buildings in the care of the Secretary of State for the Environment which are open to the public

Garden
Golf course or links
Historic house
i Information centre
Motor racing
Museum
Nature or forest trail
Nature reserve

☆ Other tourist feature
Picnic site
Preserved railway
Racecourse
Skiing
Viewpoint
Wildlife park
Zoo

𝕮𝖗𝖔𝖘𝖘
SAILING Selected places of interest
T Public Telephone
⊕ Mountain rescue post

◆ ◆ National trail or Recreational Path Long Distance Route (Scotland only)

Pennine Way Named path

NATIONAL PARK ACCESS LAND Boundary of National Park access land
Private land for which the National Park Planning Board have negotiated public access

◄ Access Point

WALKS

START Start point of walk
Featured walk
➤ Route of walk
▪▪►▪ Alternative route

SYMBOLS

Place of worship { with tower / with spire, minaret or dome / without such additions

Building; important building
Glasshouse; youth hostel
Bus or coach station
Lighthouse; beacon
Triangulation pillar
· T; A; R Telephone: public; AA; RAC
Sloping masonry
Electricity transmission line
pylon pole
○ W, Spr Well, Spring
Site of antiquity
1066 Site of battle (with date)

Gravel pit
Other pit or quarry
Sand pit
Refuse or slag heap
Loose rock
Outcrop
Cliff
Boulders
Scree

Water | Mud
Sand; sand & shingle
National Park or Forest Park Boundary
NT National Trust always open
NT National Trust limited access, observe local signs
NTS NTS National Trust for Scotland
FC Forestry Commission

ABBREVIATIONS
1 : 25 000 or 2½ INCHES to 1 MILE also 1 : 10 000 / 1 : 10 560 or 6 INCHES to 1 MILE

BP,BS	Boundary Post or Stone	Mon	Monument	Spr	Spring
CH	Club House	P	Post Office	T	Telephone, public
FV	Ferry Foot or Vehicle	Pol Sta	Police station	A,R	Telephone, AA or RAC
FB	Foot Bridge	PC	Public Convenience	TH	Town Hall
HO	House	PH	Public House	Twr	Tower
MP,MS	Mile Post or stone	Sch	School	W	Well
				Wd Pp	Wind Pump

Abbreviations applicable only to 1 : 10 000 / 1 : 10 560 or 6 INCHES to 1 MILE

Ch	Church	P	Pole or Post	TCB	Telephone Call Box
F Sta	Fire Station	PW	Place of Worship	TCP	Telephone Call Post
Fn	Fountain	S	Stone	Y	Youth Hostel
GP	Guide Post				

Walk location map

Rivers and valleys
1 King's Caple, Sellack and Hoarwithy
2 Ashford in the Water and Monsal Dale
3 Postbridge, Laughter Hole and Bellever
4 Widbrook Common and Cliveden Reach
5 Bidford-on-Avon, Cleeve Prior and
   Middle Littleton
6 Bolton Abbey, Barden Tower and the Strid

Woods and forests
7 Hospital Lochan, Glencoe
8 New Fancy and Mallards Pike Lake
9 Aldbury, Ivinghoe Beacon and Ashridge
10 Knightwood Oak and New Forest reptiliary
11 Shugborough Park, Sherbrook valley and
   Brocton Coppice
12 Leith Hill and Friday Street

Lowlands
13 Calbourne
14 Killin – Finlarig and Loch Tay
15 Walberswick marshes and common
16 Tenterden
17 Elterwater and Skelwith Bridge

Moors and downs
18 Abbotsbury and Chesil Beach
19 Hole of Horcum
20 Yearning Saddle and Deal's Hill
21 Dunstable Downs
22 County Gate, Brendon and Malmsmead Hill
23 Devil's Dyke

Cliffs and beaches
24 Zennor to St Ives by the Tinners' Way
25 Wooltack Point and Marloes
26 Robin Hood's Bay and Ravenscar
27 Friston Forest, the Seven Sisters and
   Cuckmere Haven
28 Sheringham Park and Pretty Corner
29 Craster and Dunstanburgh Castle

Hills and mountains
30 Ashness Bridge, Watendlath and Bowder Stone
31 Great Malvern and the Worcestershire Beacon
32 Birks of Aberfeldy
33 Broadway and Broadway Tower
34 Fan y Big and Taf Fechan Forest

Heritage walks
35 Cerne Abbas and Minterne Magna
36 Hadrian's Wall from Steel Rigg
37 Tintern Abbey and the Devil's Pulpit
38 Carreg Cennen Castle
39 Constable Country
40 Ribblehead and Chapel le Dale

Walks on the wild side
41 The Glyders
42 Hartside, Salters Road and High Cantle
43 Helvellyn
44 Ben Nevis

Rivers and valleys

Walking in river valleys in some ways offers the best of all worlds, often combining both upland and lowland walking. An ideal walk has the outward route along the side or top edge of a valley and the return by the riverbank, thus getting the most strenuous part, the climb onto the valley slopes, over first. The views are varied and often stunning throughout.

The rivers of Britain are a varied collection and flow through widely contrasting terrain. Upland and moorland rivers can be spectacular after rain, surging over boulders through wild landscape and steep-sided valleys. Some of the most delightful riverside walking is in the limestone dales of Yorkshire and Derbyshire and such walks are included in the following selection. The walks by the Wye and Warwickshire's Avon, two of our best-loved rivers, illustrate classic English riverside scenery, with gently sloping, well-wooded country with fields, orchards and villages and dotted with church towers. Any selection of riverside walks must include England's most famous river and the walk by the Thames follows one of its finest reaches below the thickly wooded cliffs of Cliveden.

In the past rivers were the main means of communication and major trade arteries. Many of our earliest settlements grew up along their banks and important towns developed at river crossings. Riverside walks are therefore likely to pass through attractive old villages and traditional market towns, often with fine churches and other interesting buildings, and as an added bonus plenty of pubs and tearooms.

FLORA AND FAUNA

Many rivers start life as bubbling, hillside streams which are the haunt of the dipper and where common sandpipers bob in the gravelly shallows as they collect grubs and snails.

Later, in flatter terrain, rivers may meander through wooded valleys or flow slowly past water-meadows, alight in summer with meadowsweet and pink valerian. Dragonflies hover above the colourful herbage over which yellow wagtails *(above)* proceed in looping flight before diving into the lush vegetation to reach their well-hidden broods.

Bolton Abbey, Barden
Tower and the Strid ●

● Ashford in the Water
and Monsal Dale

Bidford-on-Avon, Cleeve
Prior and Middle Littleton
●

King's Caple, Sellack ●
and Hoarwithy

Widbrook Common
and Cliveden Reach ●

● Postbridge, Laughter
Hole and Bellever

King's Caple, Sellack and Hoarwithy

There can be few short walks more pleasant than this gentle stroll through one of the loveliest stretches of the Wye Valley which reveals English riverside scenery at its finest: an intimate patchwork of fields and orchards, rolling hills and woodland, delightful riverside meadows and quiet old villages. The route passes through three of the latter, each with highly distinctive churches, and for most of the way the spire of King's Caple church, the starting point, is in sight.

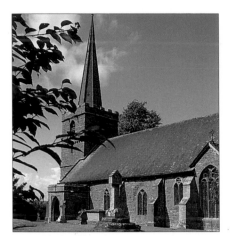

King's Caple church, built of red sandstone

Start	King's Caple church
Distance	5 miles (8 km)
Approximate time	2½ hours
Parking	Wide verges near King's Caple church
Refreshments	Pub at Hoarwithy
Ordnance Survey maps	Landrangers 149 (Hereford & Leominster) and 162 (Gloucester & Forest of Dean), Pathfinder 1064, SO 42/52 (Ross-on-Wye (West))

Start by King's Caple church, the first of three interesting village churches that can be visited on this walk. A handsome building occupying an elevated position above the valley, it is built of the local red sandstone. It is a harmonious mixture of styles, ranging mainly from the twelfth to the fifteenth centuries, and is dominated by the fourteenth-century tower and spire, a landmark for miles around. The mound on the opposite side of the road is Caple Tump, site of an early motte and bailey castle.

With your back to the church, turn left along the lane through the small village, passing an orchard on the right. Keep ahead at a crossroads and about 50 yards (46 km) after passing a school on the left turn right along a tarmac drive **A** signposted to Seven Acres. After a further 50 yards (46 km) bear right onto a track with granite chippings to go through a metal gate and climb a stile beside another metal gate a few yards ahead.

Bear slightly right and head across the field to a fence corner, here veering left to walk along the field edge, by a wire fence on the left, down to a stile. From here there are extensive views ahead over the Wye Valley with the spire of Sellack church prominent. Climb the stile, continue in the same direction along a narrow path, now by the right-hand edge of a field and with a wire fence and hedge on the right. Where the hedge and fence turn to the right, keep straight ahead across a cultivated field, turning left at the bottom end for a few yards to a metal gate and footpath sign. Go through the gate and turn right along a lane to where it bends to the right, here turning left through a metal gate **B**. Continue along a hedge-lined path to cross a rather shaky suspension bridge over the River Wye, built in 1895 to replace an earlier ford and ferry – hence the name Sellack Boat on the map.

Walk across the meadow ahead in the direction of Sellack church, crossing a footbridge over a ditch and continuing across this expanse of meadowland to go through a metal gate beside the church **C**. This is another attractive old sandstone building with a fine fourteenth-century spire. The village is tiny and secluded, no more than a few houses and farms.

Immediately turn right through another metal gate and head across meadows, keeping more or less in a straight line and roughly parallel with the wooded cliff of Castlemeadow Wood on the left, to reach the riverbank a short distance before a stile. Climb the stile and keep along the riverbank; this is an idyllic part of the walk as the Wye flows serenely through a lush landscape of meadows, fields of green and gold, orchards, farms and villages, with rolling wooded hills beyond and church spires punctuating the skyline. Eventually you follow a path to the left by some cottages; look out for a stile on the right and climb it onto a road.

Turn left for a few yards and take the first turning on the right **D**, signposted to Kynaston and Hentland, following a road gently uphill for ½ mile (0.75 km) to where it bends sharply to the left. Here turn right at a public footpath sign, along a hedge-lined track **E**, and where the track bends left in front of a pylon keep ahead along a grassy enclosed path, which may be

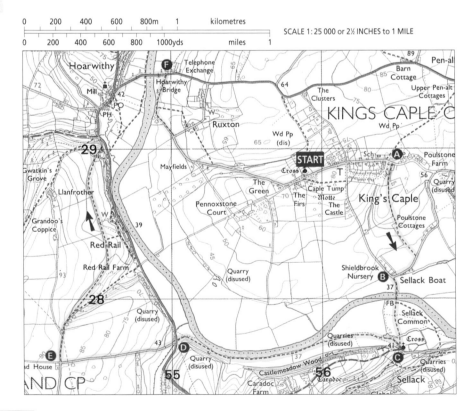

0 200 400 600 800m 1 kilometres
0 200 400 600 800 1000yds miles 1

SCALE 1: 25 000 or 2½ INCHES to 1 MILE

overgrown, to a stile. Climb it and continue along the left-hand edge of a field, by a hedge and wire fence on the left. There are more superb views over the valley, with the spire of King's Caple church the dominant feature. Go over a stile into a long field, still keeping ahead with the hedge to the left. At the bottom left-hand corner of the field there is another stile. Climb it and cross straight over the track which faces you, passing to the left of a house called Quarry Bank, and continue downhill along a delightful, if in places overgrown, tree-enclosed path to a road. Follow the road through the village of Hoarwithy, bearing right at a junction in the direction of King's Caple.

To the left is Hoarwithy church, which you reach by climbing some steps. Its Italian design could hardly look more incongruous in this quintessentially English setting. The reason why such an unusual, highly ornate and richly decorated church came to be built here is that the local vicar, William Poole, felt that its predecessor was too plain and therefore used some of his great personal fortune to finance the construction of this lavish replacement in 1885. It took over twenty years to finish and Poole even employed Italian craftsmen to achieve the desired effect. One feature that it has in common with the churches at King's Caple and Sellack, however, is that it is built of the local sandstone.

Continue across the bridge over the Wye and on the other side turn right along a grassy, hedge- and tree-lined track **F**, which shortly meets and keeps by the river for a while, before curving left away from it to reach a lane. Follow the lane for nearly ¾ mile (1.25 km) back to King's Caple church. □

Classic English riverside scenery at its finest makes this a delightful walk. This tranquil stretch of the Wye is near Hoarwithy

Ashford in the Water and Monsal Dale

A walk such as this, which combines one of the most idyllic villages and one of the finest viewpoints in the Peak District, superb woodland and some lovely stretches of riverside walking in Monsal Dale, is bound to be an intensely pleasurable and memorable experience. Good clear footpaths, two gradual ascents and a modest distance make it an easy walk, and it is one worth taking plenty of time over.

Start	Ashford in the Water
Distance	6 miles (9.5 km)
Approximate time	3 hours
Parking	Ashford in the Water
Refreshments	Pubs and cafés in Ashford, pub and café at Monsal Head
Ordnance Survey maps	Landranger 119 (Buxton, Matlock & Dovedale), Outdoor Leisure 24 (The Peak District – White Peak area)

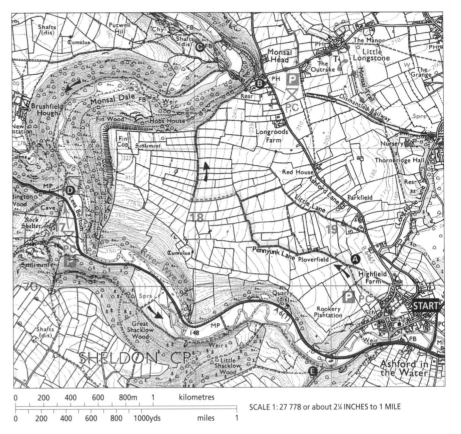

0   200   400   600   800m   1   kilometres
0   200   400   600   800   1000yds   miles   1

SCALE 1:27 778 or about 2¼ INCHES to 1 MILE

Ashford in the Water is an exceptionally attractive village, its mainly eighteenth- and nineteenth-century limestone cottages situated amidst meadowland and clustered around the church, which was largely rebuilt in the late nineteenth century. The water of the title is the River Wye and the name of the village means exactly what it says – a ford near ash trees. The ford was an important link in an ancient routeway called the Old Portway, but was superseded in the seventeenth century by the construction of a three-arched pack-horse bridge, the most photographed structure in Ashford. It is known as the Sheepwash Bridge because of the enclosure at one side of it, where sheep were held before being washed in the river prior to shearing. The church has two unusual features. One is the four virgin crants, decorated garlands which hang from the roof and which used to be carried in the funeral processions of unmarried girls. The second is a table of Ashford black marble, a locally quarried dark limestone which when highly polished took on a black appearance. Production of it ceased only in 1905.

From the car park behind the church walk ahead into Court Lane and turn right along Vicarage Lane. After about 50 yards (46 m) turn sharp left at a footpath sign for Monsal Dale, almost doubling back on your tracks, along a path that bears right, climbs some steps and continues up to a stile. Climb over and head across a field in a straight line, making for a stile in the top right-hand corner. Climb it and turn left along a winding, walled track **A** which gives glorious and expansive views over the surrounding countryside. Where the track ends, climb a stone stile and bear left along the edge of a field, climbing gently to another stone stile. Turn right at a footpath sign and keep ahead to join another walled track. Continue over several stiles to emerge at Monsal Head, and bear right to follow the head of the dale round to a road **B**.

The view from here is probably the finest of many fine views looking down the dale: the Wye winds gently below between meadows and the steep-sided wooded slopes of the dale, and the disused railway viaduct in the forefront of the scene appears to harmonise perfectly with its surroundings. This was not the view of Victorian conservationists led by Ruskin, who bitterly opposed the desecration of the dale by the construction of what they felt was an ugly and intrusive structure. The viaduct was part of the Bakewell–Buxton section of the Midland Railway route from St Pancras to Manchester, which opened in 1863 and closed in 1968. Nowadays part of

The old railway viaduct strides across Monsal Dale, seen here from Monsal Head

Sheep used to be washed by the attractive three-arched Sheepwash Bridge which spans the River Wye in the village of Ashford in the Water

the route forms the Monsal Trail, a footpath that almost links Buxton with Bakewell.

From the road take the path signposted 'Monsal Dale, Viaduct and Trail', and descend some steps. Keep straight ahead, ignoring the path to the left for 'Viaduct and Trail', and continue downhill between trees and shrubs. Turn left through a gate at the end of farm buildings, cross a footbridge over the River Wye and turn

left again **C**. There is now a delightful riverside walk of 1¼ miles (2 km). The path goes under the viaduct, past a weir – where the dale becomes narrower and more thickly wooded – and continues along the right-hand side of the winding river through a beautiful wooded gorge to reach the main road **D**.

Cross over, keep ahead across a car park drive and bear left along a path that heads

up to a stile. Climb over and continue, following yellow arrows, to a marker-post. Here bear left, following waymarks for Route 3, shortly afterwards turning left over a stone stile and heading uphill to another marker-post. Turn left, ascending to a stile in a wall, climb it and continue ahead into Great Shacklow Wood.

The path keeps along the side of the valley through the steep-sided wood,

gradually dropping down to join the riverbank by a former watermill that was used for crushing bones for fertiliser. Continue by the meandering Wye and over several stiles to reach a minor road **E**. Turn left, then right at the main road, and after about 300 yards (274 m) turn left over the picturesque Sheepwash Bridge back into Ashford village. Continue ahead along Fennel Street to the car park. ☐

Postbridge, Laughter Hole and Bellever

This is an ideal walk for children, with plenty of interest en route, and towards the end the chance of getting thoroughly wet in the East Dart River at Bellever! With stretches of moorland, a lovely riverside section at the start and finish and exciting stepping-stones at Laughter Hole, it also makes an excellent introduction to walking on Dartmoor.

Start	Postbridge
Distance	7½ miles (12 km)
Approximate time	4 hours
Parking	Postbridge
Refreshments	Pub at Postbridge
Ordnance Survey maps	Landranger 191 (Okehampton & North Dartmoor), Outdoor Leisure 28 (Dartmoor)

From Postbridge car park cross the bridge and take the lane on the right to Lydgate House Hotel. A pleasant alternative is to cross the clapper bridge and follow the left bank of the stream through meadows on a 'permitted path'; this path joins with the other just before the hotel driveway. The route, a blue-waymarked bridlepath, passes in front of the hotel and crosses a series of riverside meadows before bending left away from the river to climb past a hut. Turn right at the wall at the top and keep walls and fences on the left until a very

The ancient clapper bridge at Postbridge can be seen in front of the road bridge over the East Dart River at the starting point of this walk

Stepping-stones at Laughter Hole

muddy section. At the end of the track bear right. Here the track becomes a streambed; keep your feet dry by following the right-hand side of the stream to cross by a small stone clapper bridge marked by a blue-topped post. Ignore the footpath to Bellever at the top of the hill and turn left through a gate to reach Pizwell Ⓐ.

The lane winds down past the back of a house and through a former farmyard whose buildings are converted to cottages. Cross the stream at the stepping-stones to reach a level, heather-banked track which heads towards the road. Just before it reaches this turn right onto a well-used bridlepath Ⓑ. This crosses Cator Common to reach a road which crosses a belt of trees. Turn left and follow the road for about 1 mile (1·5 km), with views over the hedges of a typical Dartmoor landscape, with Yar Tor on the right. Ignore the turn to the left at Cator Green, but where the lane opens onto the moor turn right along a farm track Ⓒ. After 20 yards (18 m) a footpath sign on the left points to 'Dartmeet via Sherrill'. This path provides wonderful views to the right, and on a sunny September day the heather and gorse give off an incense-like fragrance. Climb to the signpost at the top of the wall ahead from where Yar Tor, in front, is even more distinct. The path descends to reach the road at Sherwell ('Sherrill' on some signposts) Ⓓ.

Turn right and follow the road down past Rogues Roost to Babeny. Just before

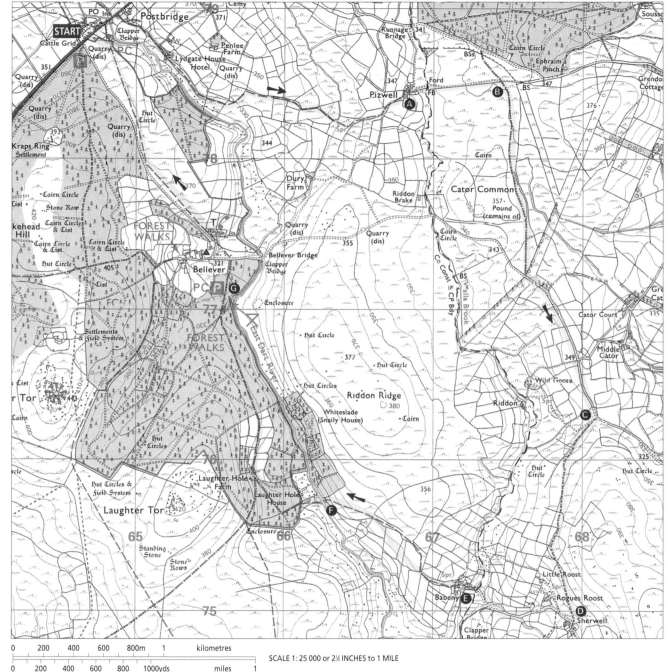

SCALE 1: 25 000 or 2½ INCHES to 1 MILE

the farm Ⓔ look for a blue-waymarked path on the right which climbs to a track behind the house. This leads to a gate onto the open moor, and then descends to the river at Laughter Hole House. Cross the East Dart by the relatively easy stepping-stones Ⓕ and climb past the left side of

the house onto a path leading through a narrow belt of forest. The ground has been cleared at the top. Turn right to Laughter Hole Farm and follow the signs through the forest to Bellever. The riverside picnic site provided by the Forestry Commission is always popular Ⓖ

The track emerges onto a road. Cross it and head diagonally for a field gate to the left of the wall ahead. Bear to the right onto a lane. When the lane is adjacent to the end of the woods on the right, after about ¾ mile (1.25 km), bear to the right off it to return to Postbridge.

Widbrook Common and Cliveden Reach

The first part of the walk to Cookham is mostly across flat, open meadow and marshland, with extensive views across the surrounding countryside. After Cookham the route heads down to the Thames and continues along Cliveden Reach, a particularly beautiful stretch of the river below the glorious hanging woods of Cliveden, to return to Boulter's Lock.

Start	Boulter's Lock, about ¾ mile (1.25 km) north of Maidenhead Bridge on A4094
Distance	5½ miles (8.75 km)
Approximate time	2½ hours
Parking	Boulter's Lock
Refreshments	Pubs and cafés at Cookham
Ordnance Survey maps	Landranger 175 (Reading & Windsor), Pathfinder 1157, SU 88/98 (Maidenhead & Marlow)

Begin by walking away from the main road and take the path that leads from the far left-hand corner of the car park to a road. Turn left to a T-junction, turn right, and just after passing a road called The Pagoda bear right along a path between fences **Ⓐ**. Where the path ends cross a road, continue along the road ahead – Summerleaze Road – following it around a left-hand bend. Where the road turns sharply to the left **Ⓑ**, turn first right and then immediately turn left over a metal stile at a public footpath sign.

Riverside meadows at Cliveden Reach

Follow the hedge-lined path ahead which bends right and continues by a wire fence bordering gravel works on the right, then bends left to a metal stile. Climb the stile, keep ahead to cross a footbridge over a small stream and continue along a grassy path by the stream on the right. On reaching a wider path just before a stile, turn right to cross first a footbridge and then a metal stile to reach a public footpath sign. Here keep ahead across the middle of a field, following the direction signposted Green-Way East, passing to the left of a line of trees and continuing to a public footpath sign at a gap in the hedge on the far side. Go through this gap and continue across the next field, bearing slightly right and then keeping by a wire fence on the right. Walk past the first footpath sign and continue to the second one by a metal stile in the field corner.

Climb the stile and bear right along a broad track. Ahead Cliveden House can be seen on its wooded cliff above the Thames and all around are extensive views across flat meadowland. At a public footpath sign just before a metal gate, turn left and follow a path straight across a large field to climb a stile at the far end, here entering Widbrook Common, an area of pasture owned by the National Trust. Keep ahead to cross a footbridge and follow a path along the left-hand edge of the common, keeping parallel to a hedge and trees on the left, to a stile in the far corner. Climb it, keep along the right-hand edge of a field, by a metal fence on the right, and at the end of the field turn right at a public footpath sign to continue along the left-

hand edge of the field, by trees on the left that border Strand Water. Keep along the left-hand edge of a second field and at the end of it cross a track, bear right to climb a stile and continue along the left-hand edge of another field, by a metal fence on the left. From here the tower of Cookham church is visible on the left and Cliveden House is ahead.

The route continues along an enclosed path which turns left to eventually emerge onto a drive at Cookham Moor on the western edge of the village. Turn right **Ⓒ**

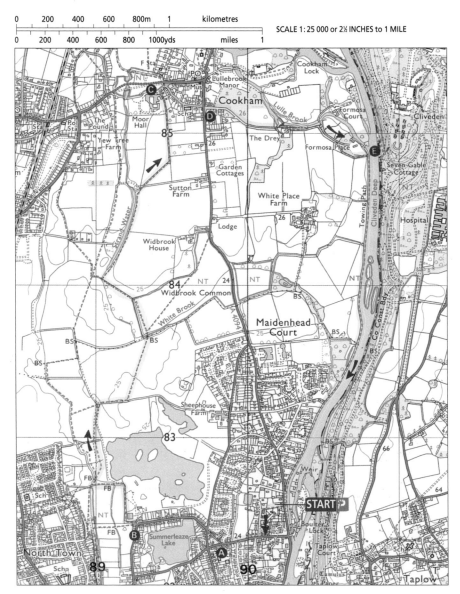

SCALE 1: 25 000 or 2½ INCHES to 1 MILE

The Thames flows serenely below the hanging woods of Cliveden – one of the most beautiful stretches of the river, which the walk follows along a tree-lined path

to the war memorial and continue along High Street to a T-junction. Cookham is an attractive riverside village with a beautiful twelfth-century church and a wealth of old buildings, many of them dating back to the seventeenth and eighteenth centuries. Stanley Spencer lived here for most of his life and many of his paintings were based on the village and local area. The Stanley Spencer Gallery is at the end of High Street.

At the T-junction turn right, then take the first turning on the left **D** – Mill Lane – and follow this winding lane for ½ mile (0.75 km). At some houses bear right, at a public footpath sign, along a hedge-lined path which curves left to a tarmac drive. Cross the drive and continue along the path opposite which winds through woodland, keeping parallel to the lane on the left, to reach the river **E**

Turn right to follow the riverside path along Cliveden Reach, an exceptionally attractive stretch of the Thames, for 1½ miles (2.5 km) back to Boulter's Lock. For most of the way the path is shady and tree-lined. To the right are extensive views across flat meadows to the wooded hills on the horizon, and to the left you pass below the hanging woods of Cliveden owned by the National Trust. Cliveden House, seen

earlier on the walk, stands 200 feet (61 m) above the river. The present house – the third on the site and built by Charles Barry in 1851 – became the property of the Astor family and was associated with the political intrigues and gatherings of the 'Cliveden Set' in the 1920s and 1930s, and later with the Profumo scandal of 1963. The path eventually emerges onto the road opposite the car park at Boulter's Lock. ☐

Bidford-on-Avon, Cleeve Prior and Middle Littleton

The route first crosses fields and meadows, passing through Marlcliff and Cleeve Prior, to the adjacent villages of North and Middle Littleton. From here a gentle climb onto a ridge is followed by a fine ridgetop walk of almost 3 miles (4.75 km) above the winding River Avon back to Marlcliff. Despite its modest height of about 220 feet (67 m) the ridge reveals outstanding views across the orchard and market-gardening country of the Vale of Evesham to Bredon Hill, the Cotswolds and the Malverns on the horizon. A final pleasant stroll is across riverside meadows back to Bidford-on-Avon.

Start	Bidford-on-Avon
Distance	8 miles (12.75 km)
Approximate time	4 hours
Parking	Bidford-on-Avon
Refreshments	Pubs and cafés at Bidford-on-Avon, pub at Cleeve Prior, pub at North Littleton
Ordnance Survey maps	Landranger 150 (Worcester & The Malverns), Pathfinders 997, SP 05/15 (Stratford-upon-Avon (West) & Alcester) and 1020, SP 04/14 (Vale of Evesham)

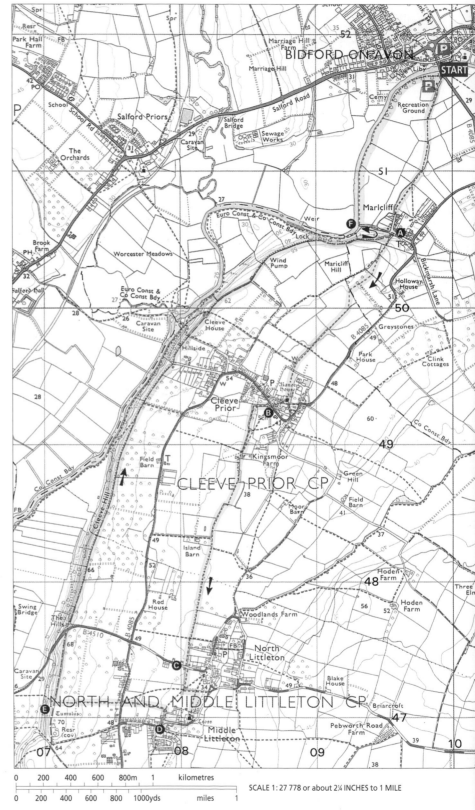

The view of Bidford-on-Avon from the river is most attractive. Houses are massed above the riverbank, with the fifteenth-century stone bridge over the River Avon in the foreground and the tower of the restored medieval church behind.

Start on the south side of the old bridge over the Avon by entering the riverside recreation ground. Bear left along its left-hand edge, by a hedge on the left, go through a kissing-gate and follow a clear path across the middle of a field to climb a stile. Continue along the left-hand edge of the next field, by a hedge on the left, turn left over a stile and ditch and walk along the right-hand edge of a field, by trees on the right. Climb another stile, keep along the right-hand edge of the next field, by a fence on the right, go through a gap and

continue between fences on both sides, over another stile and on into the village of Marlcliff, a harmonious mixture of modern houses and old black-and-white thatched cottages.

Keep ahead to join a lane and at a junction bear right **Ⓐ**, passing to the right of the thatched cottage in front. Go through a gate and follow a short but steep climb up Marlcliff Hill. At the top keep ahead across grass to climb one stile and continue across a field to climb another. Bear slightly left across the next field, climb a stile and follow a path across the next one, continuing by the left-hand edge of an orchard to pass through a hedge gap. Bear left across a field to a stile in the far corner, climb this and keep ahead, by a hedge on the right, to pass through a gap

With its fifteenth-century bridge spanning the river and its medieval church, Bidford is one of a number of attractive villages on the banks of Shakespeare's Avon

in a fence. Continue, still by a hedge on the right, cross a footbridge over a brook and bear slightly left across the next field, heading directly towards Cleeve Prior church. Climb one stile, keep ahead and climb another to enter the churchyard. Bear right to pass in front of the church, going through a metal kissing-gate and onto the road by the village green **B**.

Cleeve Prior is pleasant and sleepy, and rather like a Cotswold village with many stone houses and cottages and an impressive thirteenth- to fourteenth-century church. Cross the road and at a public footpath sign to North Littleton continue along the track opposite, which soon bends to the left at a public footpath sign to Middle Littleton. Keep along the track; at first it is hedge-lined, then it continues along the left-hand edge of a field and passes through a hedge gap.

It bears right by a line of trees on the left, turns left over a footbridge and continues along the right-hand edge of fields.

Keep in a straight line – later switching to walk along the left-hand edge of fields – to emerge eventually onto a lane on the edge of North Littleton **C**. Turn left for the pub; otherwise cross the lane and take the path ahead, between fields, turning right over a stile. Now turn left and immediately left again over another stile, keep along the edge of a field, by a hedge on the left, and where you see a stile on the left turn right and head across the field, making directly towards Middle Littleton church. The view ahead is dominated by a large tithe barn, 136 feet (41 m) long, which belonged to the monks of Evesham Abbey and is now National Trust property. Climb a stile and continue through the churchyard, passing to the left of the

church and going through a metal kissing-gate onto a lane.

Turn right and where the lane bends to the left turn right again **D**, at a public footpath sign to Cleeve Prior and a sign to the tithe barn, along a tarmac track. Climb the stile in front, turn left along the left-hand edge of a field, keeping by garden fences, climb another stile and continue, then climb a third stile onto a road. Cross over, climb the stile opposite and keep along the right-hand edge of a field, by a fence on the right. Where that fence ends continue straight ahead, climbing gently onto a ridge **E**. From this modest ridge, of only 220 feet (67 m), there is a magnificent view ahead across the Vale of Evesham, with the Avon winding below, the Malverns on the horizon and Bredon Hill and the Cotswold escarpment to the left.

Turn right and now follow a superb ridgetop walk of almost 3 miles (4.75 km) to Marlcliff. The track, which can be muddy at times, is well waymarked; it crosses one road and later a narrow lane. It is hedge- and tree-lined in places but the many gaps reveal superb views on both sides, outstanding ones to the left over the Avon valley. Eventually you descend Marlcliff Hill, bearing left through a gate into the village and momentarily rejoining the outward route **A**.

At a public bridleway sign turn left along a track to the river, and just before reaching it turn right over a footbridge to climb a waymarked stile **F**. Keep along the riverbank back to Bidford – a flat, easy stroll – climbing a series of stiles and finally following the edge of the recreation ground to return to the starting point by the bridge.

Bolton Abbey, Barden Tower and the Strid

It is no wonder that Bolton Abbey has provided inspiration for artists, including Turner. The ruins harmonise perfectly with their exquisite setting, with meadow, moorland, woodland and the great sweep of the Wharfe creating a scene of unrivalled beauty. A short distance upstream is the Strid, where the Wharfe narrows to a mere stream and plunges through a spectacular, rocky, tree-lined gorge. Still further upstream it flows below the substantial ruins of Barden Tower. All these features are combined in this splendid and sometimes dramatic walk. There is a lengthy but gradual climb at the beginning and some narrow rocky paths by the Strid but otherwise the route presents no problems.

Start	Bolton Abbey
Distance	8 miles (12.75 km)
Approximate time	4 hours
Parking	Bolton Abbey
Refreshments	Café at Bolton Abbey, restaurant at Barden Tower, café between the Strid and Bolton Abbey
Ordnance Survey maps	Landranger 104 (Leeds, Bradford & Harrogate), Outdoor Leisure 10 (Yorkshire Dales – Southern area)

From the car park turn left along the road to Burnsall and soon after passing under an eighteenth-century arch that was once an aqueduct, bear left onto a track signposted to Halton Height and Rylstone **A**. The first part of the walk, across fields, woods and moor, is easy to follow, waymarked with blue signs all the way. Pass through a gate and head across a field to a bridleway sign near a wire fence and by the side of a pond. Follow the fence, go through a gate and turn right across a field to enter a wood. In a short while take a sharp left-hand turn, following blue arrows, and continue through the wood to a gate in a wall. Go through to emerge into open country, following a line of blue stones across two large fields. There are glorious views to the right up Wharfedale.

Continue through a gate and along a path parallel to a wall on the left. The path skirts Middle Hare Head on the right and goes over the shoulder of the hill, bearing slightly right to a gate. Pass through and keep ahead to the road **B**. Turn right and follow the road downhill for 1¼ miles (2 km) to a T-junction, turning left here **C** to the remains of Barden Tower.

Barden Tower belonged to the Clifford family of nearby Skipton Castle, and was originally built in the twelfth century as one of a number of hunting lodges in the Forest of Barden. The remains mostly date from the fifteenth century, when the lodge was rebuilt and extended by the tenth

RIGHT *The ruins of Bolton Abbey harmonise with their lovely setting in Wharfedale*

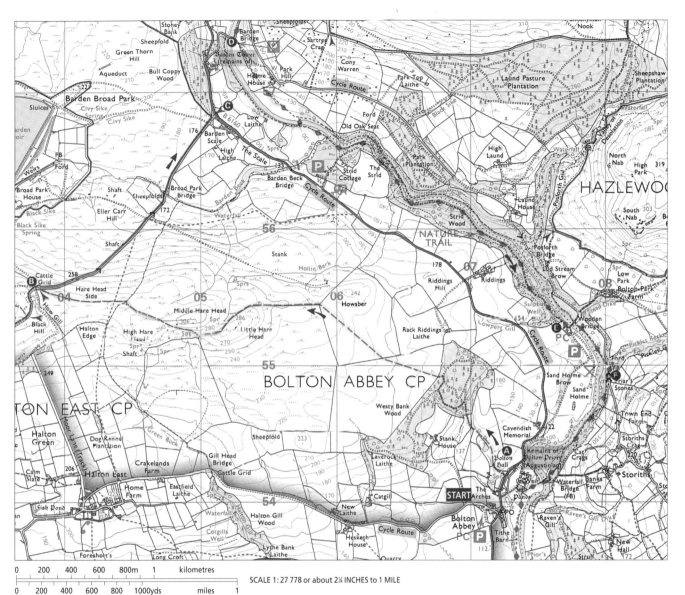

Barden Tower, a medieval hunting lodge

Pavilion café and a footbridge **E**. Cross the bridge, turn right along the other side of the river, climb a stile and turn left by a stream. Go across a minor road, cross a footbridge over the stream, keep along the road uphill for a few yards and bear right along a path to Bolton Priory **F**. This path winds through the woods above the river, giving splendid views of the great bend in the Wharfe and the priory ruins on the opposite bank, eventually dropping down to a footbridge. Cross over and walk up to the ruins.

Bolton was founded as a priory of Augustinian canons in 1154, but after its dissolution in 1539 the adjoining village and local parish became known as Bolton Abbey and this is the name which has survived. The east end of the church, rebuilt after a Scottish raid in the fourteenth century, is now ruined and is dominated by the great east window which offers views of the hills beyond. In contrast, the nave of the church survived intact, as this part was always used as the local parish church and still serves that purpose today. It is unusual in that it has two west fronts: the original thirteenth-century one and an unfinished sixteenth-century one. The latter was started only twenty years before the priory was dissolved, hence its uncompleted state. The cloisters and surrounding domestic buildings have almost entirely disappeared, apart from the fourteenth-century gatehouse, incorporated in the present, mainly Victorian, Bolton Hall.   □

Lord Clifford, the 'Shepherd Lord', who preferred the rural simplicity of Barden to his main residence at Skipton. Separate from the main block is the former chapel and priest's house, the only part not ruined, and now used as a restaurant.

From the tower continue along the road down towards Barden Bridge, and just before the bridge go through a gap in the wall on the right **D** and down some steps to join the riverside path. Now comes a superb 3-mile (4.75 km) walk, through woods and across meadows, along or

close to the banks of the Wharfe to Bolton Abbey. Soon after passing a turreted bridge, which is a Victorian aqueduct carrying water from reservoirs in Nidderdale to Bradford, cross meadows to a gate which gives access to the Strid Woods. There are a number of paths through the woods, trails laid out by the Devonshire Estates, but this route follows the path closest to the river. Take care – during wet conditions it can become slippery and quite dangerous. Eventually the Strid is reached, heralded by the noise

of the river, which at this point is only a few yards wide and surges over the rocks as it squeezes through the narrow gorge. It is a most impressive and beautiful spot and one in which to linger but, sadly, people have lost their lives here, foolishly trying to stride (Strid) across the narrow channel.

Now the path becomes much easier, broadening out into a flat and clearly defined track which keeps ahead to a junction of tracks. Here bear slightly to the right along the wider path which climbs and then descends to the Cavendish

Woods and forests

There can be few more enjoyable experiences than walking through native woodland of beech, oak and birch, especially in May when the bluebells are out or in October when the trees are resplendent in their autumn finery. Part of this enjoyment stems from the fact that many of our woodlands are remnants of the ancient forests that once stretched across much of lowland Britain and thus form an important part of our national heritage.

The ancient forests were not necessarily large, continuous areas of woodland, for in the Middle Ages forest was a legal term for the king's private hunting grounds, and could include heath, moor, marsh, farmland and villages as well as woodland. Demands for land for agriculture and settlement, and for timber for the shipbuilding and iron-smelting industries, led to the destruction of many of their woodlands, but some were replanted when timber was needed to build wooden warships for the navy – the main reason for the survival of so much of the New Forest and the Forest of Dean.

More recently the conifer plantations of the Forestry Commission have added a new and different type of woodland to the British landscape, one which can provide attractive walking, especially when planted in a more informal way and edged with native broadleaved trees. The commission lays out trails, provides picnic sites and generally encourages visitors and walkers into most of its forests, adding considerably to Britain's recreational amenities.

FLORA AND FAUNA

In early spring, when the trees in oakwoods are leafless, wood anemones and later on bluebells carpet the ground. By June, when the leafy canopy is complete, only dappled lighting illuminates the woodland floor, and while the shade is appreciated by speckled wood butterflies *(above)*, plants such as red campion now flower along the more sunny edges.

Beechwoods are probably most attractive in autumn when the leaves assume fiery, coppery shades and their nuts, falling to earth, attract flocks of chaffinches and bramblings.

• Hospital Lochan,
Glencoe

Shugborough Park,
Sherbrook valley and
Brocton Coppice
•

Aldbury, Ivinghoe
Beacon and Ashridge
New Fancy and •
Mallards Pike Lake •

Knightwood Oak and
New Forest reptiliary •
Leith Hill and
Friday Street

Hospital Lochan, Glencoe

This is a delightful walk to start or finish a day and offers a lush woodland setting, in great contrast to the ruggedness more usually encountered in Glen Coe. In early summer the rhododendrons will be in bloom, and early or late in the day the woods are fragrant and cool – and the views over loch, sea and hill are often sharper then.

Start	Glencoe village
Distance	3 miles (4.75 km)
Approximate time	2 hours
Parking	Glencoe village
Refreshments	Pubs in Glencoe village
Ordnance Survey maps	Landranger 41 (Ben Nevis & Fort William), Pathfinder 305, NN 05/15 (Glencoe)

SCALE 1: 25 000 or 2½ INCHES to 1 MILE

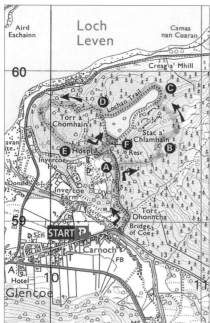

Banks of rhododendrons, magnificent in bloom in early summer, can be seen on this walk

Glencoe, the village, retains something of its ancient character, and the walk begins by heading along its one street towards the dramatic Pap of Glencoe. This was the old road through Glen Coe and you cross the River Coe by a fine humpback bridge. The Celtic cross on the right is 'In memory of Maclan, Chief of Glencoe, who fell with his people in the Massacre of Glencoe'.

Shortly after crossing the bridge turn left, up the hospital drive. When the drive forks take the right, unsurfaced track which leads to a car park Ⓐ. The Forestry Commission has created three local walks and this route more or less combines these in a single circuit.

Leave the car park by a small gate in the far corner which leads to a steep gravel path twisting up through a jungle of rhododendrons. You can see how efficiently this plant seeds; it is now a menace in many areas. There is a viewpoint and then an even steeper pull up to the top of the hill Ⓑ for an even more extensive view.

The path then descends almost as steeply and comes out onto a track beside the lochan. Turn right to walk round the end of the lochan Ⓒ, which is artificial, the work of Lord Strathcona who laid out these grounds and built the big house – now the hospital – in such a way as to try to 're-create' Canada for the sake of his half-Red-Indian wife. There is plenty of gaultheria, a Canadian flower, growing by the path.

Walk on along the far side of the lochan. There are several overgrown islets and across the 'dam' can be seen a boathouse/shelter. A path goes off to the right Ⓓ; take this for a new circuit, the Woodland Walk. Ignore the first path breaking off right, but several others, also to the right, are worth brief diversions as they lead to ever-changing viewpoints. The path switchbacks along; when it forks Ⓔ bear left and descend through another jungle of rhododendrons.

This path emerges on a big track. Turn left and walk along to an arch formed by two intertwining rowan trees – a good-luck symbol – fronting a tiny lily-pond. The track forks at the arch Ⓕ. Go right, up to the boathouse/shelter, cross the 'dam' and turn left to pass the rowans again and so back along the drive towards a white house. Just before it, about opposite where this track was joined the first time, bear sharp left along a lower track which leads to the car park Ⓐ and on to the village.

The fjord-like nature of Loch Leven is well seen on this walk. The great ridges of Beinn a' Bheithir (Ben Vair) sweep down to the sea and the Ballachulish Bridge appears a tiny link over its narrows. The islands in front include the ancient Macdonald burial site of Eilean Munde. The grounds of Lord Strathcona's house evidently failed to re-create Canada, for the couple returned to British Columbia.

Back in Glencoe village take time to visit the Glencoe and North Lorne Folk Museum. The name Glen Coe is synonymous with the Massacre of 1692 and that story is illustrated here, as is much else relating to life in the glens in times past. Three miles (4.75 km) up the glen's main road, the A82, is the National Trust for Scotland visitor centre which has interpretative displays and refreshments.

RIGHT *Wooded hills around the lochan*

New Fancy and Mallards Pike Lake

*Quiet forest tracks and pleasant glades make it difficult to believe that most
of this walk is in the vicinity of what was once a busy coal-mining area;
it crosses several of the disused railway lines that served the nearby collieries.
The route passes through mixed woodland, Mallards Pike Lake adds variety,
and either at the beginning or the end you can enjoy an extensive panoramic
view over the Forest of Dean from the top of the landscaped tip
of the former New Fancy Colliery.*

Start	Forestry Commission car park at New Fancy
Distance	4½ miles (7.25 km)
Approximate time	2½ hours
Parking	New Fancy car park
Refreshments	Pub at Moseley Green
Ordnance Survey maps	Landranger 162 (Gloucester & Forest of Dean), Outdoor Leisure 14 (Wye Valley & Forest of Dean)

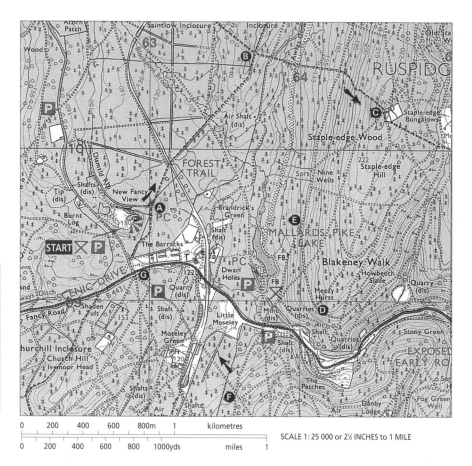

The walk begins on the site of the New
Fancy Colliery which was open from 1832
to 1944 and produced around 3½ million
tons of coal. The vast spoil heap was
partially removed in 1961 and the rest was
grassed over and landscaped in 1975 to
form a car park, picnic site and viewpoint.

From the car park follow red-
waymarked 'Forest Trail' signs, turning
right along a track that was originally a
colliery tramway. Climb a stile beside a
gate, and at a T-junction turn left along
a track bordered by a now incomplete
avenue of lime trees that were planted in

Mallards Pike Lake, created by the Forestry Commission as a recreational amenity

the early nineteenth century **Ⓐ**. Keep
ahead at a junction to cross the former
'Mineral Loop' line of the Severn & Wye
Valley Railway Company, opened in 1872
to serve the local collieries. The line was at
its peak just before the First World War,
declined in the 1920s and '30s and finally
closed in 1953.

Continue along the pleasant straight
track to the next crossroads and here
cross the track of a railway line that was
abandoned before even being completed.
This was the Forest of Dean Central
Railway, a competitor of the Severn & Wye
company, and it was because the latter's
'Mineral Loop' line won the lucrative trade
of the New Fancy Colliery that the Central
railway stopped laying its track.

Keep straight ahead along a narrow
path that heads uphill to a crossroads
of paths **Ⓑ**. Turn right, head down to
another crossroads, continue along a

path – following yellow waymarks – that
winds downhill and just after it starts to
ascend bear left at a yellow waymark.
Head gently uphill again, cross a track
and continue through the conifers,
crossing over another track and now
climbing more steeply to reach a track at
the top of the hill in front of Staple-edge
Bungalows **Ⓒ**.

Turn right along the broad main track –
there are several routes here, which can
be slightly confusing – and on reaching
the corner of the wire fence bordering
the bungalow garden on the left, bear
right off this main track over a stile
and along a pleasant grassy path. This
continues gently downhill, keeping
more or less in a straight line, through
a conifer plantation and over several
crossroads of paths to reach a broad track
Ⓓ. Turn right along it and at a T-junction
of tracks turn sharp left **Ⓔ**, almost

This panoramic view over the thickly wooded Forest of Dean is from the landscaped tip of a former colliery. The view can be enjoyed at the beginning or end of the walk

doubling back and heading downhill. The track passes the attractive, tree-fringed Mallards Pike Lake below on the right, created by the Forestry Commission in 1982 as a recreational amenity. Continue over a disused railway line in a cutting below, pass by a forestry barrier and keep ahead to a road.

Cross over and take the track straight ahead, passing by another forestry barrier and continuing to a junction of tracks just in front of an electricity pole **F**. Here turn sharp right along a track which leads to the road at Moseley Green near the Rising Sun Inn. Turn right for a few yards and then turn left along another broad, grassy

track, passing a forestry barrier and heading uphill. Keep in a straight line all the while – at first through conifers and later through an extensive area of broadleaved woodland – to reach a road junction **G**.

Take the road ahead, signposted to Speech House and Cinderford, turning along the first track on the right. Climb a

stile beside a gate and continue along the track as far as a red-waymarked post **A** where you turn left to retrace your steps to New Fancy car park. If you did not do so at the start, climb up to the viewpoint on top of the former colliery spoil heap to take in the magnificent all-round view over the densely wooded forest. ☐

Aldbury, Ivinghoe Beacon and Ashridge

This outstanding walk starts in a picturesque village, proceeds along the Chiltern escarpment to Ivinghoe Beacon – one of the highest and finest viewpoints in the Chilterns – and returns through part of the magnificent woodlands of the National Trust's extensive Ashridge Estate. There are several climbs but the paths are good throughout, the route is easy to follow, and the views are superb all the way.

Start	Aldbury
Distance	7 miles (11.25 km)
Approximate time	3½ hours
Parking	Aldbury. Alternatively, Bridgewater Monument or Pitstone Hill and start walk from there
Refreshments	Pubs at Aldbury, tearoom at Bridgewater Monument (summer weekends)
Ordnance Survey maps	Landranger 165 (Aylesbury & Leighton Buzzard), Pathfinder 1094, SP 81/91 (Aylesbury & Tring)

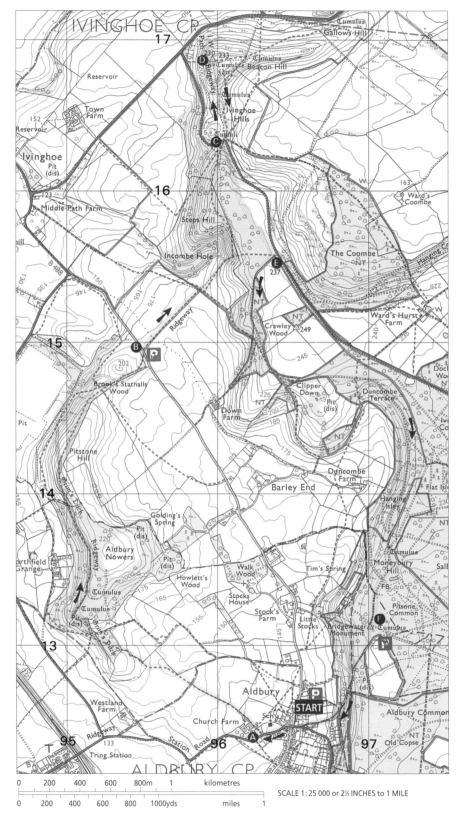

All the ingredients that make up the classic English village scene are present in Aldbury: charming brick and half-timbered cottages, some thatched, and a pub grouped around a triangular green; duckpond, stocks and whipping-post standing on the green; and a short distance away a medieval church. To enhance the scene further, the village is set against the glorious backdrop of the beech woods of Ashridge. It is not surprising that Aldbury has frequently been used as a film set.

Start by walking along the road in the Tring direction, passing the church, and at a public footpath sign to Pitstone Hill turn right over a stile **A**. Head across to climb another stile to the left of a metal gate, continue along the left-hand edge of a field, by farm buildings on the left, but before the end of them look out for and climb a stile on the left. Immediately turn right along a narrow enclosed path, climb a stile, keep ahead to climb another and continue along a path between wire fences.

Climb two stiles in quick succession and continue across part of a golf-course, following a fairly obvious grassy path and keeping in the same direction as before – a series of yellow-waymarked posts aid route-finding. Later, keep along the left edge of trees and a hedge to go through a kissing-gate in the top right-hand corner of a field, and continue between trees, bushes and scrub to reach a finger-post at a path junction. Bear left and then turn right up a flight of steps, here joining the Ridgeway.

Follow the acorn-symbol Ridgeway waymarks over Pitstone Hill. Initially the route passes through woodland, but after climbing a stile it continues over open downland with some fine views to the left over the Vale of Aylesbury, even though the dominant feature is the Pitstone cement works. The path later descends and curves gradually to the right, keeping close to a wire fence on the right, finally bearing left to a stile in front of Pitstone Hill car park.

The return part of the walk is through the glorious beech woods of Ashridge, now one of the largest and most popular National Trust properties

On this descent the escarpment and next part of the route can be seen stretching ahead to Ivinghoe Beacon.

Climb the stile, pass through the car park **B**, cross a lane and take the path opposite that heads straight across a large field. Climb another stile and continue across the next field. The path then keeps below a bank on the right, ascending and curving left to a stile. Do not climb it but pass to the left of it and head across, keeping parallel to a hedge and wire fence on the right, to a Ridgeway marker-post on the edge of woodland. Continue through the trees and on emerging from them keep ahead downhill, by a wire fence on the right. Turn right over a stile in the fence, head uphill through an area of scrub and bushes, and then continue downhill to

climb a stile. Bear left down to the corner of a road **C**. Cross the road and follow the left-hand one of the two tracks ahead up to the summit of Ivinghoe Beacon, marked by a triangulation pillar **D**. From this outlying spur of the Chiltern range, 750 feet (228 m) high, there is a magnificent panorama over the Vale of Aylesbury, along the Chiltern escarpment from Dunstable Downs to Coombe Hill and across to the slopes of Ashridge Park.

Retrace your steps to the road **C**, cross over and then turn left, at a National Trust marker-post, along a pleasant path that initially keeps parallel to the road on the left, heading uphill between trees to join a track. Bear left along the track, which curves left to reach an open grassy area beside the road. Turn right alongside

hedges on the right, parallel to the road, and at the end of this grassy area turn right along a track signposted 'Private Drive to Clipper Down Cottage and permitted footpath and bridleway to Bridgewater Monument' **E**.

Almost the whole of the remainder of the walk is through part of the splendid beech woods of the Ashridge Estate, over 4,000 acres (1,618 ha) of open grassland, commons and woodlands belonging to the National Trust. Follow the track through this attractive woodland, taking care to keep on the main track all the while, to Clipper Down Cottage. Go through a gate at a Bridgewater Monument sign, pass to the right of the cottage and continue along another track. At intervals there are superb views to the right from these wooded

slopes across the flatter country of the vale. Pass to the left of a log cabin and soon after crossing a footbridge you reach the Bridgewater Monument **F**, erected in 1832 in memory of the third Duke of Bridgewater, the great canal-builder and owner of Ashridge. The view from the top is well worth the climb.

Keep ahead past the monument to join a track in front of the National Trust shop, information centre and tearoom. Turn right and follow the track downhill through woodland; a gap on the right reveals a superb view of Aldbury village and church nestling in the valley below. At a fork take the right-hand lower track to continue downhill to a road and turn right for a short distance to return to the centre of Aldbury village. ☐

Knightwood Oak and New Forest reptiliary

This short walk visits three of the New Forest's best-known sites. From the car park it crosses a typical forest road, bordered by old and ornamental trees, to pass the Portuguese fireplace, part of the cookhouse of a Portuguese army camp in the 1914–18 war and now set beside a barbecue and picnic area. After a woodland walk to the Holiday Hill Reptiliary where examples of all the New Forest's reptiles can be seen, and a walk over a small heath, the route visits the 300-year-old Knightwood Oak, one of the most ancient trees in the New Forest.

Start	Millyford Bridge, New Forest (off A35, through Emery Down and turn left at New Forest Inn)
Distance	3½ miles (5.5 km)
Approximate time	2 hours
Parking	Forestry Commission's Millyford Bridge car park
Refreshments	None
Ordnance Survey maps	Landranger 195 (Bournemouth & Purbeck), Outdoor Leisure 22 (New Forest)

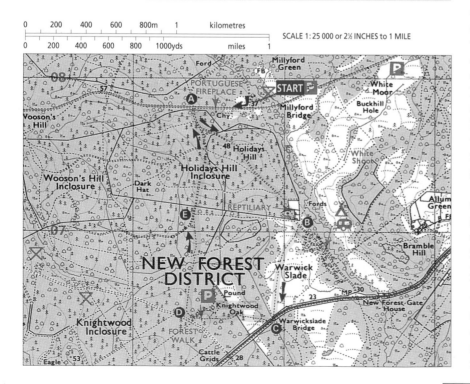

SCALE 1:25 000 or 2½ INCHES to 1 MILE

Leave Millyford Bridge car park by going back onto the road and turning right, and almost immediately there is a barbecue area on the opposite side of the road. Walk past the picnic tables to visit the Portuguese fireplace. During the First World War Portuguese troops were stationed in the New Forest to help produce vitally important timber – there was a shortage of local manpower at the time as most forest workers were doing military service. To ensure that meals were cooked in the traditional way troops constructed this fireplace, and it now stands as a memorial to their assistance. Continue ahead along the wide grass verge at the side of the road for a short distance to a five-bar gate on the left. Turn left and go through the gate into the inclosure **A**.

Follow the gravel track ahead and when it divides take the left-hand gravel track and continue ahead, ignoring minor paths to right and left, until a gate bars the way. Go through and the reptiliary is ahead. Large open-air enclosures hold examples of all the native reptiles and amphibians found in the New Forest: grass snakes, adders, slow-worms, smooth snakes, sand and common lizards, newts, common toads and frogs. All reptile numbers have declined in Britain, due mainly to loss of habitat, and smooth snakes and sand lizards are now found almost nowhere else in Britain except Dorset and the New Forest. Visitors can view some of these fascinating and shy creatures. The reptiliary also breeds rarer reptiles for release back into the forest.

Go through the gate beside the keeper's cottage, out of the reptiliary and down the gravel drive. Turn right in front of the cottage by a 'no parking' sign to take a narrow grass path that heads for a lone pine tree on the heath the house faces **B**. The path zigzags through the heather and then widens out to follow the right-hand side of Warwick Slade Heath. Continue along the path which heads for the fence and road beyond. Just before reaching the fence bear right over a footbridge **C**.

Follow the path through the bracken where it bears right, then left. A path comes in from the left, then another from the right. When a further path joins from the left bear right to head for an inclosure gate. Go through and follow the wide grass ride ahead through the trees. This soon meets a narrow gravel path; bear right onto this. Ahead, in a fenced area, is the Knightwood Oak, a pollarded oak tree over 300 years old. When it was young most trees in the New Forest were cut back to produce young branches which were probably used for fuel and charcoal. This resulted in huge trunks and short trees that took up a large area of ground, so in 1698 William III brought in an act forbidding pollarding. This helps in determining the age of the trees as most old pollarded oaks and beech in the New Forest are likely to have been planted before this act came into force. The Knightwood Oak is now surrounded by eighteen young oak trees planted to commemorate the Queen's visit in 1979. They represent the visits, from William I onwards, of eighteen reigning monarchs to the New Forest.

Go back along the gravel path to see two young, labelled oak trees presented by the Queen and the Duke of Edinburgh, then follow the path into the adjoining car park. At the entrance turn right onto the tarmac road, then almost immediately, by a fallen beech tree, turn right again onto a path that leads back into the woodland **D**. Follow this wide path which is bordered by old wellingtonias, giant conifers easily recognised by their red cork-like bark. The path goes uphill, eventually meeting a gravel track. Turn right onto this **E**.

Follow this gravel track ahead, ignoring other paths to right and left, for just over ½ mile (0.75 km) until it leaves the inclosure through the gate where you originally entered it. Walk along the wide grass verge beside the road back to the car park on the left. ☐

RIGHT *The Knightwood Oak, 300 years old*

Shugborough Park, Sherbrook valley and Brocton Coppice

A remarkable variety of scenery and a wide range of historic attractions are featured in this modest but highly attractive walk on the north-western fringes of Cannock Chase. The former embraces landscaped parkland, canal and riverside meadows, conifer forest, open heathland and the finest remaining area of traditional oakwood in the chase. The latter includes an eighteenth-century mansion, a seventeenth-century pack-horse bridge and part of a disused First World War railway.

Start	Milford Common
Distance	7 miles (11.25 km)
Approximate time	3½ hours
Parking	Milford Common
Refreshments	Pub and café at Milford Common, pub and café at Great Haywood
Ordnance Survey maps	Landrangers 127 (Stafford & Telford) and 128 (Derby & Burton upon Trent), Pathfinders 851, SK 02/12 (Abbots Bromley), 850, SJ 82/92 (Stafford) and 871, SJ 81/91 (Cannock (North))

Cannock, or Cank, Forest originally covered a large area between Stafford in the west and Tamworth in the east, and from the Trent valley in the north to Wolverhampton and Walsall in the south. It was a royal forest, but in 1290 Edward I granted part of it to the bishops of Lichfield as their private chase. In the sixteenth century ownership passed to the Paget family (later the marquises of Anglesey), who pioneered the development of the local iron industry. Demands for charcoal for iron smelting led to the felling of many of the woodlands, and much of the chase became bare heathland until the 1920s, when the Forestry Commission began large-scale conifer plantations, mostly of pine. Cannock Chase is now chiefly heath and conifer forest, but some

older broadleaved woodland remains, mostly in the area of this walk.

Start by heading across Milford Common to the main road and turn right, passing the entrance to Shugborough Hall on the left. Shortly turn left by a wall on the left, which is soon followed by a wire fence, following a path that climbs between bracken and a superb array of silver birches. Bear right at the top of the hill when the path divides, away from the railings guarding the covered reservoir. Then keep in a straight line ahead, descending to rejoin the road. Turn left along it for about ¼ mile (0.5 km), and at a public bridleway sign to Great Haywood turn left through a gate **Ⓐ**, pass through another about 50 yards (46 m) further on and continue straight ahead along a

tarmac drive across Shugborough Park, which is now owned by the National Trust and administered by Staffordshire County Council although part of the house is still occupied by the Earl of Lichfield.

To the left is a view of the Anson Arch, built to commemorate the circumnavigation of the world by Admiral George Anson in the 1740s. It was largely from the profits of this voyage that George's brother, Thomas Anson, an ancestor of the present Earl of Lichfield, was able to landscape the park and enlarge and complete the house.

Cross a railway line and where the drive divides take the left-hand fork, passing to

the right of Park Farm, which is now a farm museum. Soon elegant Shugborough Hall can be seen to the left; where the main drive bears left towards it go through a gate and continue straight ahead along a narrower track to reach the seventeenth-century Essex Bridge over the River Trent **Ⓑ**. This fourteen-arched bridge was built by an earl of Essex to allow easier access to the chase for his hunting parties. Cross it and here the route turns right, along the towpath of the Trent and Mersey Canal, but a brief detour ahead over the canal bridge and under a railway bridge leads into the village of Great Haywood.

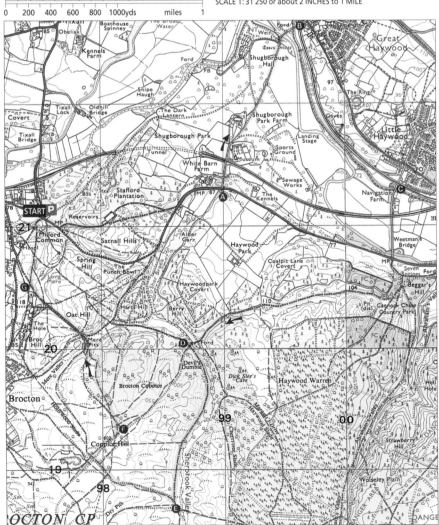

SCALE 1 : 31 250 or about 2 INCHES to 1 MILE

An attractive tree-lined track in Cannock Chase, formerly a royal forest and once the hunting ground of the bishops of Lichfield

The towpath makes very pleasant walking, initially squeezing between the river on the right and the canal on the left, with fine views across meadows looking towards Shugborough Hall. After passing under a road bridge leave the canal by climbing some steps on the right and turning left along the road **C**, following it under the railway and over the Trent to meet the main road again. Cross over and take the track ahead, which leads uphill into woodland to the pleasant parking and picnic area of Seven Springs. Here turn right, passing a forestry barrier, and where the track forks a few yards ahead take the right-hand broader track. Bear right at the next fork and continue

along an undulating track through a mixed area of heathland, broadleaved woodland and conifer plantations. Eventually the track descends gently into the Sherbrook valley at the 'Stepping Stones', an idyllic spot of widely scattered trees interspersed with grassy glades and surrounded by wooded slopes.

Cross the brook by the stepping-stones and turn left onto the Staffordshire Way **D** to walk through the delightful Sherbrook valley; the woodland later gives way to more open country of bracken- and heather-covered slopes dotted with random groups of trees. It is easy to see why this is considered to be the most beautiful valley in the chase. Ignore the

first broad track on the right and about 250 yards (228 m) further on – by a picnic area and a Staffordshire Way sign – turn sharp right along a track **E** which soon curves to the left and heads uphill between banks of heather and bracken.

At the top the track curves to the right to continue to a forestry barrier and on to a broad track beyond. Turn right, passing through a car park, and pass another forestry barrier, ignoring the left-hand turn just past it, and continue to where the track forks **F**. At this point turn left along another track which heads downhill between the ancient oaks of Brocton Coppice, the most extensive area of oak forest remaining in Cannock Chase.

Eventually turn left to join a broad track and turn right along it as it curves above Mere Pool on the left. This track was once part of the 'Tackeroo Railway', built in the First World War to carry supplies to the two huge military camps established at the time on the chase. At a crossroads of several tracks and paths keep straight ahead, following directions to Milford, through a deep cutting. The track continues to a road, but before reaching it – soon after passing a forestry barrier – bear right onto a track **G** which heads steadily uphill, passing to the left of a small pool. At the top there is a fine view ahead over the Trent valley before you descend gently back to Milford Common. ☐

Leith Hill and Friday Street

At 965 feet (294 m) Leith Hill is not only the highest point in Surrey but also the highest in south-east England. It is a magnificent viewpoint, one of a series that crown the well-wooded greensand ridge a few miles south of the North Downs. This walk is mostly through the lovely pine and beech woods and over areas of sandy heathland that is characteristic of greensand country, and although fairly hilly in places it is relatively undemanding. However, do follow the route instructions carefully; the large number of tracks and paths in this area, much of which is owned by the National Trust, can be confusing at times.

Start	National Trust's Landslip car park below Leith Hill, near Coldharbour village
Distance	6½ miles (10.5 km)
Approximate time	3½ hours
Parking	Landslip car park
Refreshments	Pub at Friday Street, kiosk at Leith Hill Tower (weekends)
Ordnance Survey maps	Landranger 187 (Dorking, Reigate & Crawley), Pathfinder 1226, TQ 04/14 (Dorking)

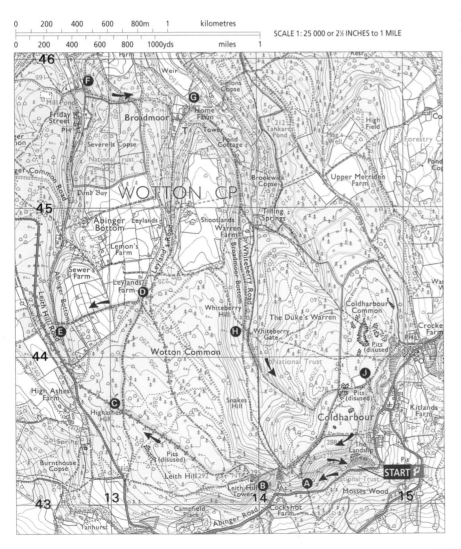

Begin by taking a path that leads up from the car park, following the first of a series of signs with a tower symbol on them, towards Leith Hill Tower. At a track turn right to head quite steeply uphill, keep ahead at a junction **A** and continue slightly downhill. Bear left in front of a gate marked 'bridleway' at a junction and climb again to reach Leith Hill Tower **B**. This was built in 1766 by Richard Hull of nearby Leith Hill Place to compensate for the hill just failing to top the 1,000-foot (305 m) mark; the extra height of the tower pushes it to 1,029 feet (313 m). From here there is one of the finest and most extensive panoramas in the south-east:

northwards across to the North Downs and beyond that to London and the Chilterns, and southwards over the Weald to the South Downs and the English Channel.

Just past the tower the path forks. Take the right-hand path here, at a second fork take the left-hand one and at a third fork take the left-hand one again. Shortly after, a well-defined path joins from the left. Continue ahead for about ½ mile (0.75 km) following the straight main path across Wotton Common to reach a crosstrack **C**. Turn right here along a fairly straight path and after ½ mile (0.75 km) bear left at a T-junction to a lane **D**. Turn left and almost immediately right, at a public footpath sign, along a path that keeps along the inside edge of woodland, with a fence on the right.

On the edge of the woodland go through a fence gap and follow a path across a field. Continue along an enclosed path to the right of houses, soon re-entering woodland, and descend, by a wire fence on the left, to a crosstrack **E**. Turn right along a track that winds through the beautiful woodlands of Abinger Bottom, briefly emerging from the trees to reach a lane. Keep ahead along the lane and opposite the drive to a house called St Johns bear right to continue along a wooded track. After passing a barrier the track becomes a tarmac lane; follow this

The secluded hamlet of Friday Street in the Surrey woodlands

From the wooded slopes of Leith Hill there are splendid and extensive views over the Weald looking towards the South Downs

through the charming and secluded hamlet of Friday Street to a T-junction.

Turn right to pass across the end of the millpond, a former hammer pond and one of many in the area that were created to power the hammers of the local ironworks up to the time of the Industrial Revolution. The view across it nowadays could hardly be more tranquil. On the far side turn half-right, at a public footpath sign **F**, along a path that heads uphill away from the pond, passing to the left of a National Trust sign for Severells Copse, and continue steadily uphill to a lane. Cross over, keep ahead to

cross another lane and continue along the path in front. Take the right-hand path at a fork – not easy to spot – and head downhill along a sunken path, bearing slightly right on meeting another path to continue downhill, curving left to a lane.

Turn left through Broadmoor, another attractive and secluded hamlet, and opposite a riding centre turn sharp right at Greensand Way and public bridleway waymarks, onto a track **G**. Keep on this straight, broad track through Broadmoor Bottom for 1 mile (1.5 km) and just over ¼ mile (0.5 km) after passing to the right of

Warren Farm, look out for a crossroads of paths and tracks by a bench **H**. Turn half-left here onto a path; after a few yards cross a stream, by a National Trust sign for Duke's Warren, and a few yards further on at a fork take the right-hand path. This is a most delightful part of the walk, initially between woodland on the right and open sloping heathland dotted with trees on the left, and later the path re-enters woodland and heads steadily uphill, finally curving left to a junction.

Bear left for a few yards to a fork and take the right-hand track, following the

direction of a blue waymark, to emerge alongside the right-hand edge of the cricket pitch on Coldharbour Common. Just after the end of the cricket pitch turn sharp right to continue along a path which has a wooden footpath post **J**, ignoring all side turns and following the main path all the while. To the left there are grand views over the Weald to the South Downs on the horizon. Opposite a barrier on the right **A**, turn left to rejoin the outward route and head downhill back to Landslip car park, following footpath signs with a car symbol with the letter 'L' on them. □

Lowlands

Lowland walking might be regarded as the Cinderella among walking categories. But while it lacks the obvious challenges and the more dramatic landscapes of mountain, hill, moorland and coastal regions, it has many compensations and undoubted attractions.

Expansive views and wide horizons are an inspiring feature of many lowland walks, greater distances can be covered, easy accessibility and the relatively low level of physical fitness required means that more people of all ages can enjoy them – and at any time of year and in almost any kind of

weather. It should, however, be borne in mind that walking in low-level, especially arable, country is likely to involve negotiating more stiles and gates, and route directions may be more complex. And in winter or wet weather paths and tracks get churned up by animals and farm vehicles – and this means mud!

Three of the five walks featured here are in the traditional lowland areas of eastern and southern England. The inclusion of a woodland and waterfall walk in the Lake District and a lochside

walk in the Scottish Highlands may come as something of a surprise, but easy, low-level walks are not confined to the more usual flat and gently rolling landscapes. Such walks among hilly and mountainous terrain provide the opportunity to enjoy the surrounding majestic scenery without a great deal of physical exertion.

FLORA AND FAUNA

Wayside banks change during the year. Early golden-flowered celandines *(above)* are superceded by loose clumps of stitchwort. Later these too will be overwhelmed, this time by rank grass from which sturdy stems of cow parsley project, each one capped by an umbrella-like cluster of flowers. Creatures such as hedgehogs can rest unseen within this mini jungle.

Hedgerow bushes also undergo a seasonal transformation. The hawthorn's May blossom gives rise to autumn's crop of berries, vital food for thrushes and blackbirds, and for winter-visiting redwings.

● Killin – Finlarig and Loch Tay

● Elterwater and Skelwith Bridge

Walberswick marshes and common ●

Tenterden ●

Calbourne ●

Calbourne

This is a perfect short walk for all the family as there is something to interest everyone, especially children. Starting at a picturesque working watermill the route follows a stream, the Caul Bourne, as it winds through the lush pastoral countryside of the north-west of the Isle of Wight to flow past Winkle Street in Calbourne, one of the island's most attractive villages. Pleasant field paths and green lanes complete the circle back to the mill where there is much to see and enjoy.

Calbourne watermill in its wooded setting

Start	Calbourne Mill
Distance	3 miles (4.75 km)
Approximate time	1½ hours
Parking	Car park beside Calbourne Mill
Refreshments	Tearooms at Calbourne Mill, pub in Calbourne village
Ordnance Survey maps	Landranger 196 (The Solent), Outdoor Leisure 29 (Isle of Wight)

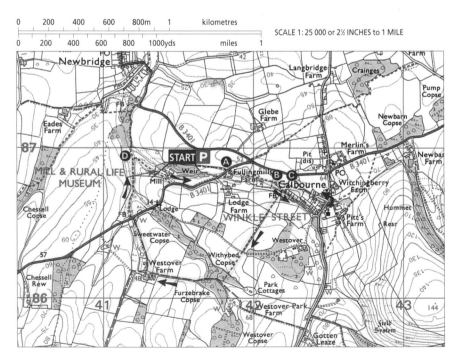

The fertile soil of this part of the Isle of Wight produces a wealth of meadow flowers and grasses which sometimes overgrow footpaths. Signposts can be concealed in the flourishing hedgerows, so navigate carefully. Part of the return route could have boggy patches but should not present any real difficulties.

Calbourne watermill is beautifully set in a wooded valley threaded by the Caul Bourne stream which rises nearby in Westover Park. There was a mill on the site when Domesday Book was compiled; the mill was valued at six shillings and three pence (31.25p). The present mill buildings date from the seventeenth century, and the machinery is in perfect working order. Visitors can wander throughout the mill and watch its great overshot wheel, 20 feet (6 m) in diameter, operating the two pairs of grindstones which produce flour for the café's home-baked goodies. Fascinating displays of farm and domestic bygones are housed in some of the mill outbuildings, and children will enjoy feeding the tame waterbirds, which range from magnificent peacocks to families of affectionate ducks that roam around the landscaped grounds.

From the mill car park turn left, with the Caul Bourne valley on the left, and walk along the grass verge of the B3401 road for about 400 yards (366 m). Just past a group of farm buildings look carefully for a flight of stone steps up the bank on the right **A**. Climb them and then climb the stile to follow the field path ahead. Fullingmills Farm is beside the stream on the right. This was originally one of six fulling mills on the island which processed kersey, a narrow, rough cloth made from locally produced wool. For centuries wool was one of the mainstays of the island economy.

When the hedge ends on the right continue straight on over the field to a stile. Climb it, go over the track ahead, and keep on over stiles and fields until you come to double stiles **B**. Climb these. There is no clear path at this point, so bear a little to the right diagonally over the field to the streamside. Climb the stile to the left of the stream to a good path running along the bank. Follow this leafy way as it emerges from the wood and suddenly becomes Winkle Street. This picturesque row of eighteenth-century stone cottages overlooking a stream bordered with flowers, ferns and lawns must be the most photographed scene on the island. After passing the cottages the stream narrows to fall noisily between two large shaped and grooved stones. Until 1975 this was a sheepwash, used by all the local farmers, boards being placed in the grooves to control the depth of the water. A plaque beside the stones gives some interesting details. Evidently in the mid seventeenth century an attempt was made by the owner of Westover Park to make farmers pay for this privilege. The indignant farmers took the case to law and won.

Continue to the bridge at the end of the street from where there is a good view on the right of Westover Park, a fine Regency house. Turn left to follow the road through Calbourne village. On the right is the church, also mentioned in Domesday Book. Inside there is a fine brass dating from 1579. It commemorates William Montacute, a son of the Earl of Salisbury, who while jousting with his father was accidentally killed by his father's lance. Heartbroken, the earl ordered a brass of his son to be placed in every church which stood on his lands.

A little further along the street, opposite a well under a tiled roof, turn left down School Lane. The lane bears left past the Old School House and continues to the recreation ground. Keep straight on, with a fence on the left, to climb a stile. Keep ahead over the next field to climb another stile **C**. There is no clear path at this point. Bear left to cross the track followed earlier in the walk, towards the Caul Bourne. Go over the footbridge and climb the stiles to follow the path ahead as it bears a little to the right, away from the hedge. Keep straight on now, over stiles and fields towards the middle of a small wood, Withybed Copse, which soon appears ahead. At the approach to the wood climb the stile and follow the path

The Caul Bourne flows past picturesque thatched cottages at Winkle Street in Calbourne, one of the most attractive villages on the Isle of Wight

as it dips over a stream and climbs through the trees to a stile leading to a good track. Turn right towards Westover Farm. On the left unfold wide views of undulating farmland, curving towards the thickly wooded slopes of Brighstone Down.

In front of the farm turn right to follow the lane past a thatched lodge. Cross the B3401 road, climb double stiles and keep ahead along a shallow valley with a tributary of the Caul Bourne on the right. Keep along the valley – there may be some

boggy patches – until you see a stile ahead. The path back to Calbourne Mill is to the right about 50 yards (46 m) before the stile, but it is very faint. To make certain of the correct route continue to the stile **D**, do not climb it but turn right and follow the

streamside, with the stream on the left, for about 50 yards (46 m) to join the path to the mill. Turn left to follow the path over the stream and walk up the field ahead, bearing a little to the right to a stile which leads to Calbourne Mill car park. ☐

Killin – Finlarig and Loch Tay

This level walk follows the line of the old railway which once ran from the village to a pier at the head of Loch Tay where passengers would disembark onto a steamer. From the loch the return walk is by loch- and riverside meadows to Killin, which means 'long village' – it extends for more than 1 mile (1.5 km). This makes a relaxing evening stroll, though the meadows may be wet after prolonged rain.

Start	Killin
Distance	2 miles (3.25 km)
Approximate time	1 hour
Parking	Municipal car park at north end of village
Refreshments	Pubs and tearooms in Killin
Ordnance Survey maps	Landranger 51 (Loch Tay), Pathfinder 334, NN 43/53 (Killin)

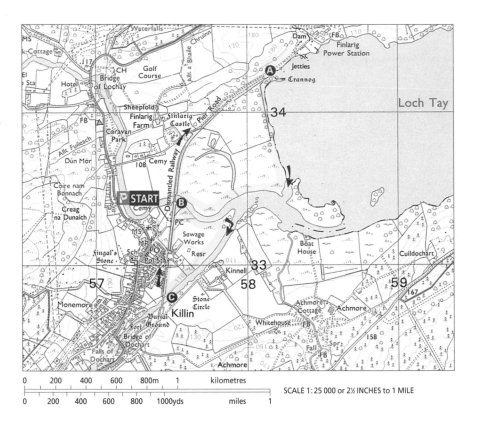

SCALE 1:25 000 or 2½ INCHES to 1 MILE

A blend of highland and lowland scenery – the River Lochay near the start of the walk

The old railway which once linked Killin with a steamer pier is now a public walkway and can be joined at the car park. Turn north (left) onto its trackbed and cross the iron bridge over the River Lochay. Meall Garbh is the splendid mountain dominating the landscape ahead.

Trees effectively hide the ruins of Finlarig Castle, on a hillock on the left, which was the headquarters of the Campbells in Breadalbane after they bought the Auchmore lands in the fifteenth century. A gruesome feature of the ruins is the 'beheading pit' where the Campbells disposed of prisoners they were unable to ransom. Before the Campbells came to the district this was MacNab land and the MacNabs continued to live here, uneasily, after they had finally mortgaged most of their estate to the sixth laird in 1553. The MacNabs lived in a fine house close to the castle and their relationship with their powerful neighbours was ever stormy. General Monk had to intervene to prevent violence between them during the Commonwealth.

Beyond Finlarig the track runs on an embankment parallel to a road on its left. On the right there are disused telegraph poles in the undergrowth and occasionally there are old sleepers underfoot. Gradually the shore of the loch draws nearer. Turn off the railway track through a kissing-gate on the right **A** to reach a lovely path which follows the edge of the loch. The shoreline is fringed by sandy beaches backed by grand trees, many of them oaks. There is

a richly wooded island where the two rivers flow into Loch Tay, and here the path turns westwards to return to the bridge crossed earlier.

Recross the bridge and turn left off the old railway track **B** to follow another riverbank path to reach the mouth of the River Dochart. The water-meadows support a great variety of wildlife – dippers and waders can be seen in the river, while hares enjoy grazing the rich grassland.

All too soon the path reaches the old railway again, this time by an imposing masonry bridge **C**. The five arches are of concrete, one of the first examples in Britain of this material's use in such work. Turn back from the bridge along the old railway to reach the car park, diverting briefly from the track to pass through the site of the station, which was later used as a cattle market.

RIGHT *The famous Falls of Dochart at the entrance to Killin village*

Walberswick marshes and common

Bracing sea breezes may well be the most memorable feature of this walk, though the return is inland through salt marshes and reedbed to heathland, where the path uses a section of the trackbed of the old Halesworth to Southwold railway, closed many years ago. Birdwatchers will particularly enjoy the path through the marshes, the home or resting place of many interesting species, including marsh and hen harriers and bearded tits.

Start	Walberswick
Distance	5 miles (8 km)
Approximate time	2 hours
Parking	Ferry Road car park at Walberswick
Refreshments	Pubs and café at Walberswick
Ordnance Survey maps	Landranger 156 (Saxmundham & Aldeburgh), Pathfinder 966, TM 47/57 (Southwold & Halesworth)

A ruined drainage mill on the marshes

Follow the River Blyth seaward from the Ferry Road car park and turn southwards on reaching the shore. Although the beach at Walberswick is mainly of stone and shingle there is usually some smooth sand to walk on. A great bank of sand has been bulldozed into place between shore and marsh to act as a sea defence. The Dunwich River – which was crossed by footbridge soon after the start of the walk – flows through the marshes a little way inland from the bank.

The tower of St Andrew's Church can be seen dominating the village of Walberswick. Much of the church was pulled down when the prosperity of the village declined in the seventeenth century. Ahead lies Dunwich, hardly a village now but in medieval times a busy seaport with 5,000 inhabitants. In 1326 much of the town was swept away overnight by a terrible storm which also blocked off its harbour.

Turn inland from the shore **A** when nearly opposite Dingle Great Hill, a tongue of land striking into the marshes. The path follows the right-hand side of a creek, heading towards a sailless windmill – since it crosses part of the nature reserve dogs should be on leads. The reeds here are a valuable crop, harvested by machinery. Much more enduring than straw thatch, roofs made of Suffolk reed are to be found all over southern England.

The path joins with another near the windmill after crossing the Dunwich River;

bear right here. This path comes from Newdelight Walks, about 3 miles (4.75 km) inland, and is a wonderful right of way passing through marshy woodland and a vast reedbed. This is certainly a difficult path for twitchers to resist when there are such rarities as the bittern, with its unmistakable booming call, living here. Turn left at the next footpath junction **B**, leaving the bank of the river to head across the marsh towards East Hill.

A very short climb takes the path from reedbed to heathland and onto a sandy track which threads through clumps of broom, gorse and bramble to reach a tarmac road. Cross this and bear slightly left to cross East Sheep Walk and reach

a shelter belt of Scots pines and birches. Near the end of this, fork right towards Eastwoodlodge Farm and join the main road. Turn right and pass the farm, and then turn left off the road through a farm gate into a meadow **C**. The path runs parallel to the old Southwold & Halesworth Light Railway track, heading towards the town, with the water-tower and lighthouses as distinctive landmarks. This railway had a charming eccentricity, which may have been partly due to its rolling stock which had been built for the Emperor of China but was never delivered. The outlines of imperial dragons were dimly visible under the Southwold & Halesworth paintwork.

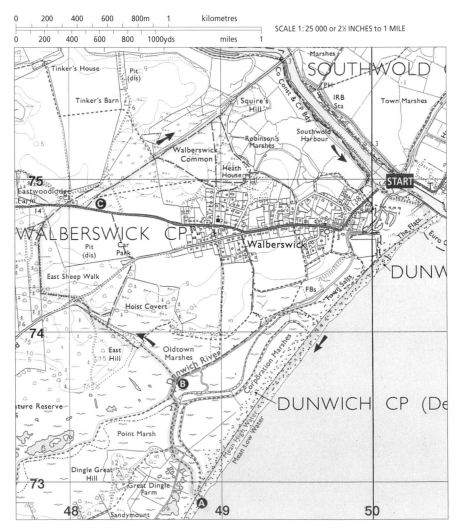

The footpath continues through a metal gate. Take the left-hand path which passes through an old cutting of the railway; it becomes very busy with walkers as it approaches the bridge at Southwold harbour. Do not cross this but turn right onto the riverbank path past small boats tied to rickety-looking stagings.

The inhabitants of Walberswick used to be known as 'Walberswick Whisperers' because of their loud voices – a result of their having to shout across expanses of reedy marshland. In summer a ferry operates across the river to Southwold from a staging at the end of the riverside path, which returns to the starting point.   □

The last stretch of the walk follows the path along the River Blyth to its mouth at Walberswick. Southwold can be seen on the opposite bank

Tenterden

This short walk goes through countryside that is typical of west Kent, with orchards, woodlands and valleys. The beautiful lake at Ashenden and the lovely buildings grouped around the ponds at Forstal Farm are picturesque features of the route.

The wide main street at Tenterden is lined with attractive old buildings

Start	Tenterden
Distance	4 miles (6.5 km)
Approximate time	2½ hours
Parking	Tenterden
Refreshments	Pubs and cafés at Tenterden
Ordnance Survey maps	Landranger 189 (Ashford & Romney Marsh), Pathfinder 1250, TQ 83/93 (Tenterden)

The walk starts at the entrance to Bells Lane, an alleyway next to the Eight Bells pub on the main street opposite the parish church. Although narrow at first the lane soon broadens as it passes bungalows and houses. Beyond these it becomes narrow again, a tarmac path which finally crosses a meadow to reach the B2082 road.

Bear left onto this, taking great care as the road is unrestricted and the traffic fast. There is a fine unrestored oast-house at Ratsbury, on the left, and at the corner here a footpath leaves to the left. Do not take this one but walk a few yards further

SCALE 1 : 25 000 or 2½ INCHES to 1 MILE

to a stile in the hedge on the left leading into a field partly planted with fruit trees. Cross this diagonally and then cross a stile and a plank bridge. Turn left by the hedge and, following a waymark post set in the hedge, bear to the right along the edge of an orchard, passing to the right of a pond.

At the start of a concrete drive at the end of the farmyard **Ⓐ** look ahead and slightly to the left to see another waymark post directing walkers to the left, through an orchard. Cross the stile at the end of the orchard and cross the following meadow. The next field may be cultivated but should be crossed diagonally to the right-hand corner where it joins another right of way just above Ashenden. Descend the bank to the drive below and bear left to walk below grassy slopes. Where these end a lovely view over a wooded valley opens up.

The driveway becomes a track as it descends into the valley with its beautiful lake. Follow the track to the bottom and then turn sharply to the left **Ⓑ** to cross a footbridge over a stream and walk back to the lake, climbing its bank onto the path which runs along its south-western shore. This is a delightful part of the walk and you may well see a heron here.

At the end of the lake the path continues along the wooded valley, which is home to large numbers of pheasants as well as grey squirrels. The path soon comes to a lovely meadow; after this cross a footbridge and turn right **Ⓒ** to climb away from the stream and reach a stile onto a track which leads steeply uphill

with woods to the right. The gradient later eases and the track is concreted up to a gate at Forstal Farm, beyond which there is a lovely scene with an oast-house and a half-timbered cottage set close together in a meadow, their rich colours reflected in two ponds. Follow the track through this meadow, past the ponds, but before a gate bear left to find a stile **Ⓓ** in the hedge close to the second pond.

Turn left after climbing the stile and walk along the edge of two fields. Cross another stile and a plank bridge over a dry ditch, and Tenterden church can be seen ahead. Turn right after the bridge for 50 yards (46 m) and then bear left to cross the neck of a field on a clear path. Another stile and plank bridge follow and after these climb up the right-hand side of the field towards the houses at the top.

Cross a final stile and bear left to cross a lane and continue along the path, which passes behind the houses. It carries on behind more modern houses further on to reach a footbridge over a stream. Follow the narrow enclosed path on the other side to a lane behind Tenterden Leisure Centre. Turn right onto the lane and just beyond the leisure centre take a footpath on the left to cross the recreation ground and the road to the leisure centre to reach Bells Lane and the starting point of the walk, Tenterden church. □

RIGHT *This oast-house at Forstal Farm is now an attractive home*

Elterwater and Skelwith Bridge

This is mainly a low-level walk, with just a few modest climbs, through a pleasant landscape of fields, woods and waterfalls at the lower end of the two Langdales, with the Langdale and Coniston Fells forming a strikingly rugged backcloth throughout. Two attractive waterfalls are passed and towards the end is one of the Lake District's classic views, looking across Elter Water to the distinctive outline of the Langdale Pikes.

Start	Elterwater
Distance	6 miles (9.5 km)
Approximate time	3 hours
Parking	Elterwater village. Alternative parking areas on common land just north of village
Refreshments	Pub at Elterwater, pub and café at Skelwith Bridge
Ordnance Survey maps	Landranger 90 (Penrith, Keswick & Ambleside), Outdoor Leisure 7 (The English Lakes – South Eastern area)

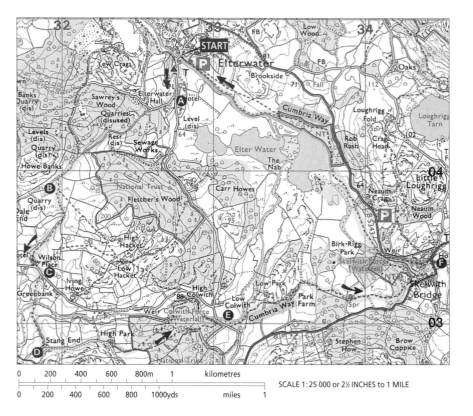

SCALE 1: 25 000 or 2½ INCHES to 1 MILE

The pleasant Langdale village of Elterwater lies scattered around a small green beside Great Langdale Beck on the edge of open common land. Just to the east is the lake of the same name, a small reedy lake whose name comes from the Norse word 'elptar', meaning swan, hence 'lake of the swans', an apt name as it is still regularly visited by whooper swans from Siberia. The walk begins by crossing the bridge over the beck and taking the Coniston road. By the Eltermere Hotel on the left turn right along a narrow lane **A** and keep ahead, climbing quite steeply up what soon becomes a stony track. The track climbs past woodland, emerging into more open country at the top, where there is a superb view ahead over Little Langdale to the Coniston Fells.

At this point turn left off the main track through a gate **B** and walk across a field, dropping down to a stone stile. Climb it, keep ahead to another one, climb that and continue along the edge of a field, dropping into Little Langdale. Go through

a farmyard, continue to a road, turn left along it for a short distance and then turn right through a gate **C**, at a public footpath sign; continue downhill to a footbridge over the River Brathay. Cross over, keep straight ahead to a stile, climb that and continue uphill to Stang End Farm **D**.

Turn left past the house along a tarmac lane, with lovely views on the left of the wooded valley of the Brathay and the fells behind. At a farm keep ahead through the farmyard (where the tarmac lane bends right), bear right through a waymarked gate at the end, head across to a second gate, go through and keep by a wall on the left to a third gate. Pass through that into the beautiful Colwith Woods and at a path junction take the left-hand fork downhill towards the river. Follow its banks to Colwith Force, a delightful fall set in woodland, where the Brathay drops about 40 ft (12 m). Continue by the river through the woods to a road **E**.

Turn right and after about 100 yards (91 m) cross a beck and turn left over a stone stile, at a public footpath sign for Skelwith Bridge. Cross a field, heading towards some trees, climb a stile and head steeply up through the woods. Climb another stile at the top, and with glorious views of Great Langdale in front follow the path ahead up to a farm. Go through a gate, over the farm track, over a fence opposite and continue ahead to a stile. Climb it, keep ahead to another stile, climb that and continue to Park Farm, passing through the middle of the farm buildings. Keep ahead, bear right at a public footpath sign, and follow a winding path past another farm, bearing left at a fork in the path by a tree and continuing down through woods to a gate. A few yards ahead turn left down the road into Skelwith Bridge.

Cross the bridge and immediately turn left at a public footpath sign to Elterwater **F**. Walk past the showroom of the Kirkstone Slate Galleries, through the

middle of the quarry yard where locally quarried green slate is processed and sold, and keep ahead along a riverside path. Soon you come to Skelwith Force, where a viewing platform is provided. Here the river narrows and falls 16 ft (5 m) over a rocky ledge; although the fall is not high it is most impressive as the combined waters from Great and Little Langdale surge through this narrow gap. Keep along the riverside path, go through a gate and continue across meadows, by the shores of Elter Water and through woods, keeping in a virtually straight line back to Elterwater village. The path is easy to follow and all along it there are spectacular views of the Langdale Pikes, especially from the lakeshore, where the sight of the twin pikes, framed by trees and with the waters of the lake in the foreground, is one of the truly memorable Lakeland views. ☐

RIGHT *The superb view looking towards the Langdale Pikes from Skelwith Bridge*

Moors and downs

Moorlands in the north and west and downlands in the south and east of Britain are very different in their geology, climate and landscape but both have a similar appeal to walkers. This is predominantly a feeling of openness and spaciousness, and an exhilarating sense of freedom.

Moors are among the last areas of wilderness left in Britain, places where you can roam all day without meeting another person. They are impressive at any time of year but look their best in late summer and early autumn when the heather is out and the ground is carpeted with great expanses of mauve and pink. But as with all wilderness areas moors must be treated with caution. In bad weather they can look forbidding and featureless, and with few obvious landmarks route finding in misty conditions is extremely difficult.

In comparison the chalk downs of the south and east are much gentler and more intensively farmed, and their smooth, grassy slopes pose few hazards. Many ridge walks along the downs have splendid and extensive views.

The following selection includes two moorland walks in the north and one in the south-west, and downland walks in Dorset, on the South Downs in Sussex and on the escarpment of the Chilterns. All provide fine walking, superb and extensive views and a feeling of remoteness – even though the latter walk is not far from busy towns and noisy motorways.

FLORA AND FAUNA

Heather, growing in acid soil, dominates the moorland scene, and grouse feed on the tender young shoots. Bracken may replace the heather where there has been over-grazing by sheep. Elsewhere, white-tufted cotton grass marks boggy areas and curlews *(above)* nest on the adjacent damp grassland.

Downland soils are not acidic and usually they are well drained. The rich sward includes many lime-loving plants such as the common rockrose and the green-winged orchid. Butterflies are frequently abundant.

● Yearning Saddle and Deel's Hill

Hole of Horcum ●

Dunstable Downs
●

County Gate, Brendon and Malmsmead Hill ●

● Devil's Dyke

●
Abbotsbury and Chesil Beach

Abbotsbury and Chesil Beach

From Abbotsbury the route climbs onto the open and windswept downs for a glorious scenic ridge walk of just over 1 mile (1.5 km) to the prehistoric fort of Abbotsbury Castle. After a descent across fields to the coast there is a walk beside the geological phenomenon of Chesil Beach back to Abbotsbury. Towards the end is an optional diversion involving a climb to St Catherine's Chapel, well worth the effort for the architectural and historic appeal of the chapel as well as the splendid view over Abbotsbury. Downland and coast, prehistoric fort and Chesil Beach, together with the monastic associations of Abbotsbury – abbey remains, tithe barn, chapel and swannery – create a fascinating and absorbing walk.

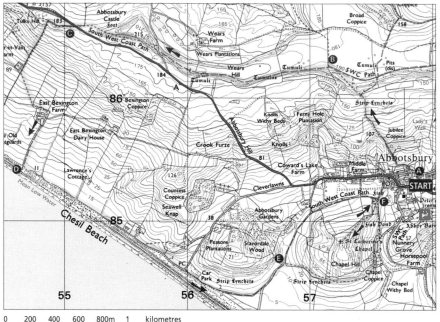

SCALE 1:31 250 or about 2 INCHES to 1 MILE

Start	Abbotsbury
Distance	6 miles (9.5 km)
Approximate time	3 hours
Parking	Abbotsbury
Refreshments	Pubs and cafés at Abbotsbury
Ordnance Survey maps	Landranger 194 (Dorchester & Weymouth), Outdoor Leisure 15 (Purbeck & South Dorset), Pathfinder 1331, SY 58 (Abbotsbury)

Little remains of the former monastic greatness of Abbotsbury except for the fourteenth-century tithe barn, 270 feet (82 m) long and claimed to be the largest in the country, and St Catherine's Chapel on a hill above the village. Of the great Benedictine abbey itself, founded in the early eleventh century, there is not much to see apart from a gatehouse. But there is the fine church, built mainly in the fifteenth and sixteenth centuries next to the abbey. The village itself has attractive, warm-looking stone houses and cottages, many of them thatched, beautifully situated in a fold in the downs and about 1 mile (1.5 km) from the sea. A further monastic survival is the famous swannery to the south of the village, established by the monks in the fourteenth century.

Start in the village centre at the junction of Rodden Row, Church Street and Market Street. Walk along Market Street, take the first turning on the right (Back Street) and after 200 yards (183 m) turn left along a track running between

St Catherine's Chapel, above Abbotsbury

thatched cottages **Ⓐ**. Turn left at a fork and head gently uphill between hedge-banks on either side. The track turns sharply to the right and continues more steeply uphill, going through one metal gate and ahead to another one.

From this gate there is a superb view behind of Abbotsbury village, church, tithe barn and St Catherine's Chapel. Go through the gate, keep ahead across a field, making for a gate and finger-post in a hedge. Go through the gate and bear slightly left, following signs to 'Hill Fort', to continue uphill along a grassy path between outcrops of rock. Keep in a straight line, heading towards another finger-post at the top of the ridge **Ⓑ**.

Here turn left to join the inland section of the Dorset Coast Path and keep alongside a wire fence on the right. Continue along this superb path that runs across the top of the broad, grassy ridge, with magnificent views to the left over the coast and to the right over rolling downland. You pass by several tumuli – be careful at one stage to ignore a track that bears left to the road below – to reach

a stile at a lane. Climb it, cross the lane and keep ahead at a footpath sign to West Bexington, climbing between gorse bushes and over a stile, then bearing slightly right to the earthworks of Abbotsbury Castle, a triangular Iron Age hill-fort commanding extensive views over downs and coast from its height of 705 feet (215 m). The path follows the line of the outer ramparts and eventually descends along a narrowing ridge before continuing over a grassy knoll, keeping parallel to the road on the left, to go through a gate in the far corner of a field to join the road **Ⓒ**.

Cross the road, climb a stile at a National Trust sign to Tulk's Hill, and continue by a wall on the left to where it ends at a finger-post. Here turn left, following directions to Chesil Beach, and head downhill along a grassy path between a wire fence and line of trees on the left and gorse and scrub on the right. A few yards after the end of the fence on the left, at another finger-post, turn left along a grassy path between scrub, soon picking up and keeping by a wire fence on the left, to a stile. Climb it and continue along the left-hand edge of a field, by a wire fence and hedge on the left, bearing left to climb a stile at the bottom end.

Bear right to follow the direction of a yellow waymark across a field, heading towards East Bexington Farm and going through a metal gate in the bottom corner of the field. Follow the track ahead through another metal gate and continue, passing to the left of the farm buildings and curving right to cross a track. Keeping straight ahead, go through a metal gate and follow the track along the right-hand edge of a field, heading directly towards the sea.

On reaching the coast turn left, in the direction signposted 'Coast Path and Abbotsbury', along a rough tarmac track **D**. Follow the track, which later becomes a tarmac lane, for 1 mile (1.5 km), at first

above Chesil Beach and later below the shingle embankment. Chesil Beach is a long, narrow embankment of pebbles and shingle, about 60 feet (18 m) above the sea at its highest point, stretching eastwards to the Isle of Portland. Beyond Abbotsbury it encloses a salt-water lagoon called the Fleet. The formation of this geological curiosity is something of a puzzle.

At the point where the tarmac lane turns to the left, keep ahead to pass beside a metal gate next to a car park and continue along a shingle path with a hedge on the left. Go through a gate and continue, between a hedge on the left and a wire fence on the right, along a track that runs along the edge of the Fleet Sanctuary Nature Reserve. Follow the track as it turns left to head inland and directly in front is a good view of St Catherine's Chapel. Ignore

a green-arrowed permissive path on the right, and at the next finger-post turn right over a stile **E**, signposted 'Coast Path and Swannery', and walk uphill across a field, heading towards and then keeping by a wire fence on the right, to a gate. Go through and follow the grassy path ahead, with a fine view to the right of the swannery below and across the Fleet to Chesil Beach. Bear slightly left to climb a stile and continue along a delightful path below a wooded hill on the left, climbing a stile at the end of the trees.

Continue along the path to Abbotsbury and just before reaching a metal kissing-gate **F** turn sharp left to follow the clearly defined uphill track to St Catherine's Chapel, a ½-mile (0.75 km) diversion worthwhile both for the chapel itself and for the views from its hilltop site.

The chapel was built around 1400 by the monks of Abbotsbury Abbey and was probably used by visitors as a place of prayer before they descended to the abbey itself. After the dissolution of the monasteries the chapel was retained, probably because of its value as a landmark for sailors. It has an almost fortress-like appearance with great buttresses, and it is noted for its rare, stone, tunnel-vaulted roof. The all-round views are magnificent, especially looking towards Abbotsbury below, cradled amidst the downs and dominated by its church.

From the chapel retrace your steps downhill to rejoin the main route and go through the metal kissing-gate **F**. Continue along a broad track to a road, turn right and take the first turning on the right to return to the starting point. □

The Dorset downs sweep down to Chesil Beach near the village of Abbotsbury, an important monastic centre in the Middle Ages

Hole of Horcum

The walk begins from a fine vantage point above the great natural amphitheatre of the Hole of Horcum and follows moorland tracks along its rim to the village of Levisham. From there it descends through woodland and returns along the valley of Levisham Beck. The views are spectacular all the way and the only steep climb comes right at the end in order to get back to the top edge of the 'Hole'.

Start	Car park on A169 above Hole of Horcum about ½ mile (0.75 km) south of Saltergate Inn
Distance	7 miles (11.25 km)
Approximate time	3½ hours
Parking	Hole of Horcum
Refreshments	Pub at Levisham
Ordnance Survey maps	Landrangers 94 (Whitby) and 100 (Malton & Pickering), Outdoor Leisure 27 (North York Moors – Eastern area)

From the car park there is an outstanding view ahead over the Hole of Horcum, one of many on this walk. Although ancient local folk-tales attribute its creation to a giant who scooped out the 'Hole' to make his home in it, the steep, smooth-sided ravine was formed as a result of erosion by escaping torrents of melt-water from the great ice-blocked lake which filled Esk Dale towards the end of the Ice Age.

Turn right and walk along the main road in the Whitby direction, following it as it curves to the left. At a sharp right-hand bend **A** keep ahead to an adjacent gate and stile. Go through the gate and continue along the broad main track, from where there are fine views to the right over Lockton High Moor and Fylingdales Moor. The track heads across heathery moorland above the Hole of Horcum, curving

gradually to the left all the while. It passes two ponds on the right – an unusual feature on these well-drained moors. The first is Seavy Pond, after which the track crosses an Iron Age dyke and continues to Dundale Pond **B**. A stone in the ground indicates that this was probably made in the thirteenth century by the monks of

The wooded track leading down from the rim of the Hole of Horcum

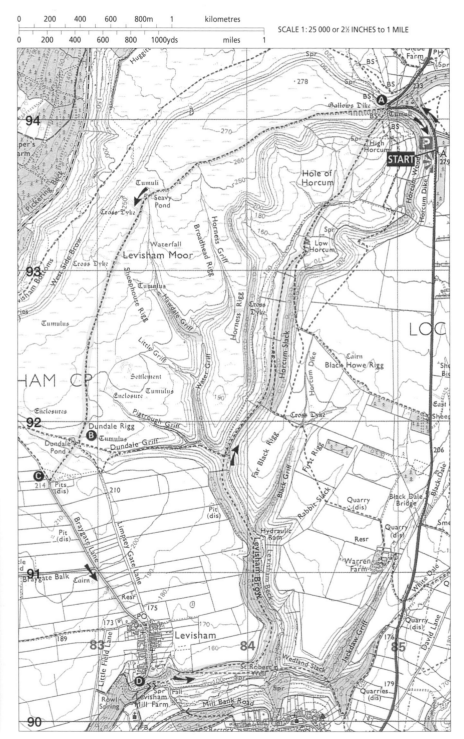

Malton Priory, who owned the land and used it as pasture for their sheep, cattle and horses. Dundale Pond is a meeting place of tracks; here bear slightly right uphill to a stile **C**. Climb it and continue along the broad, walled track ahead – Braygate Lane – which later joins a road and descends into Levisham – a remote, pretty, one-street village with a wide green lined with cottages and a pub.

At the bottom end of the village turn left at a footpath sign with a white arrow **D**, beside a bench, along a path that heads down through trees and bushes above the steep-sided valley on the right. The path then climbs some steps and follows the side of the valley round to the left, descending again through woodland and continuing above Levisham Beck. Eventually it

emerges from the trees and drops down, through a gate, to join the beck at a crossroads of paths.

Cross a tributary beck, then cross Levisham Beck by a footbridge a few yards ahead and bear slightly left, between the beck on the left and a wall on the right, to a stile. Climb it, keep ahead and continue by a wire fence on the right. Where the fence turns a corner continue straight

across the middle of a field, with woods on the right and the beck on the left, to Low Horcum Farm. Keep to the left of the farm and continue along a path which heads across grass to a gate and stile. Climb the stile to start the ascent up the side of the Hole of Horcum to a ladder-stile at the top edge. Climb that, continue a few yards to the road and bear right back to the car park. □

The natural amphitheatre of the Hole of Horcum provides outstanding moorland walking and fine views

Yearning Saddle and Deel's Hill

The path by the lovely Blind Burn leads to the mountain shelter on Yearning Saddle, a welcome refuge for those trekking along the border ridge on the Pennine Way. There are seemingly infinite views into Scotland from the northern side of the ridge. The route then follows the Pennine Way over lonely moorland to Brownhart Law before heading back over Deel's Hill to Buckham's Bridge. This is an invigorating highland walk without being too strenuous.

Start	Blindburn Bridge, 8 miles (12.75 km) up the Coquet valley from Alwinton
Distance	7½ miles (12 km)
Approximate time	4 hours
Parking	Off road near Blindburn Bridge
Refreshments	None
Ordnance Survey maps	Landranger 80 (Cheviot Hills & Kielder Forest), Pathfinders 486, NT 61/71 (Chesters & Hownam), 487, NY 81/91 (Cheviot Hills, Central) and 498, NT 60/70 (Catcleugh)

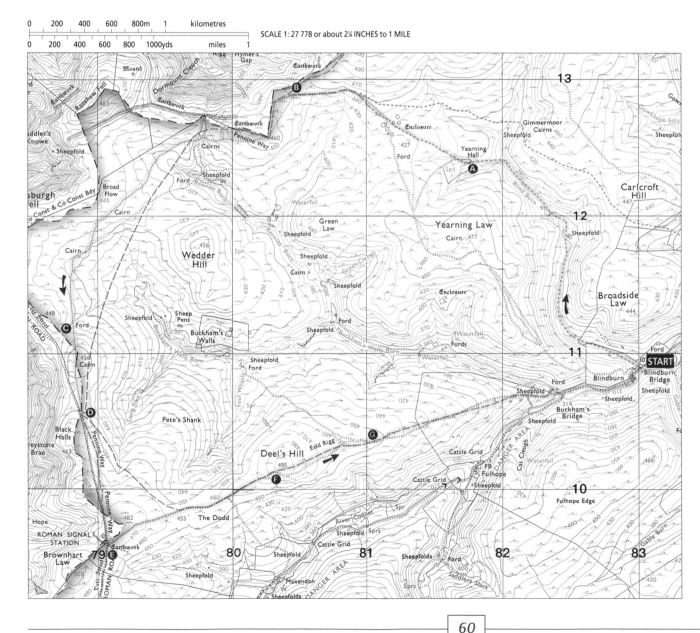

SCALE 1:27 778 or about 2¼ INCHES to 1 MILE

From the bridge take the path on the west side of the stream, the Blind Burn. Cross the stream over a plank bridge after 300 yards (274 m) and then continue on this side along an excellent path. Dippers and herons will often be seen here. Pass a military sign which warns that this is an uncleared area; the path is safe, however, and sheep safely graze on the supposedly hazardous ground on either side. Unfortunately horse-riders often use this footpath and because of this in places it is in danger of becoming broken up and boggy.

Cross a stream coming down from Gimmermoor Cairns and then there is a steep climb to Yearning Hall **Ⓐ**, the site of a ruinous croft surrounded by a few weather-beaten pines. The name 'Yearning' is said to derive from the Anglo-Saxon 'erne', a word often given to soaring birds of prey. In the past this area is likely to have been the hunting ground of white-tailed as well as golden eagles, though the latter are rarely seen in the Cheviots today. The white-tailed eagle became extinct in Britain about seventy years ago.

The climb is less demanding beyond Yearning Hall. The path, such as it is, goes past an ancient circular enclosure from where a post should be seen ahead; this points ahead to Rennies Burn. Take the other direction offered, turning right for the border ridge. This proves to be a well-used track which winds round to reach the mountain shelter at Yearning Saddle **Ⓑ**.

Few landscapes can be so devoid of human habitation as those of the high Cheviots. This is the view eastwards from Deel's Hill

There are superb views from here if you step a few yards into Scotland. The Kip is the summit with a pyramid on top.

The Pennine Way keeps the fence at a little distance to the right; this section over bleak moorland may not be very interesting – there are no views into Scotland – but it is typical of much of the long-distance path. A causeway of duckboarding takes it across the head of Buckham's Walls Burn

C. The path returns to the border ridge at Black Halls, from where there is a fine view westwards. There is no sign of the path on the left **D** across the heathery wastes to the Dodd and Deel's Hill, and it is better to continue another ½ mile (0.75 km) to Brownhart Law.

At the second of two footpath-type gates in the fence, just after the path passes through a sort of cutting, take the faint track on the left **E**; the fence changes direction at this point. (The Pennine Way continues towards a signpost in the near distance on top of a small hillock, marked on the map as a Roman signal station.)

Soon there is a valley on the right and a rounded hill ahead with a forest beyond, slightly to its right. When the track divides **F** take the path to the left leading over Deel's Hill. There is a lovely view from the top. The path now heads towards the forest and soon passes a footpath junction **G** where the path on the left is waymarked to Buckham's Walls. There is now lovely turf underfoot. A strange standing-stone of black rock can be seen on the right before the path reaches the road at Buckham's Bridge. Continue eastwards along it by the infant waters of the Coquet to reach Blindburn Bridge.

Dunstable Downs

The Dunstable Downs form part of the steep western escarpment of the Chiltern range, and from their open, grassy and often windy slopes there are extensive views over the Vale of Aylesbury and further afield towards the flat country bordering the East Midlands and East Anglia. From the visitor centre on top of the downs the route heads across pleasant, undulating country to Whipsnade Heath, and passes by the unusual 'Tree Cathedral' at Whipsnade before returning to the edge of the escarpment. The finale is a splendid 1-mile (1.5 km) ramble along the crest of the downs with grand views all the while. This is a well-waymarked walk as it follows one of Bedfordshire County Council's 'Circular Routes'.

Start	Robertson Corner, Dunstable Downs visitor centre
Distance	4½ miles (7.25 km)
Approximate time	2½ hours
Parking	Dunstable Downs visitor centre
Refreshments	Kiosk at visitor centre, pubs at Whipsnade
Ordnance Survey maps	Landranger 166 (Luton & Hertford), Pathfinders 1094, SP 81/91 (Aylesbury & Tring) and 1095, TL 01/11 (Harpenden)

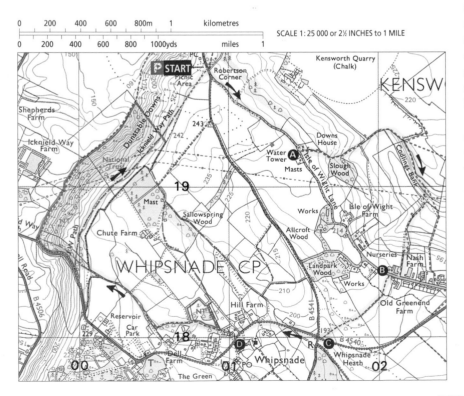

From the visitor centre turn right along the road to the point where it forks at Robertson Corner. A monument here reveals how this road junction got its name: two brothers called Robertson were killed in the First World War and a third brother gave the surrounding land to the National Trust as a memorial. At the fork take the left-hand road, pass the entrance to Kensworth Quarry, and after ½ mile (0.75 km) – just after passing a house and before reaching a radio mast – turn left through a gap in a hedge Ⓐ

Walk along the left-hand edge of a field, by a hedge on the left, and in the field corner keep ahead through trees and then continue along the right-hand edge of the next field, by a hedge on the right, heading downhill. Just before reaching the bottom corner of the field, turn right and then immediately left to walk along a track, keeping right at a fork and continuing, by a hedge and line of trees on the left, towards Kensworth Quarry. Look out for a yellow waymark which directs you to the right to continue along a pleasant path through a belt of trees. Climb a stile on the edge of the trees, keep ahead across a sloping field, just below the steepest part of the slope on the left, climb another stile and bear slightly right to head downhill across the next field to climb a stile in the bottom corner.

Turn right to walk along the right-hand edge of a field, by a hedge on the right. Climb a stile, pass to the left of a barn, turn right over another stile in front of a gate and then turn left to continue in the same direction as before, along a track that heads uphill to a cattle-grid. Keep along a hedge-lined track, and just before reaching a barn and metal gate turn left over a stile in the hedge and continue along a narrow path, climbing a stile onto a road.

Turn right, and at a public footpath sign turn left over a stile Ⓑ and walk across the middle of a field, passing a solitary tree, to a stile. Climb the stile and walk along a narrow path, between a hedge on the left and a wire fence on the right. Pass

through a wooden barrier on the edge of trees and continue through some attractive woodland to go through another barrier on the far side. Keep ahead across Whipsnade Heath car park to a road Ⓒ

Turn right, keep ahead at a crossroads and continue along the road into Whipsnade village – the road is busy but there is a verge for most of the way. Continue along the right-hand edge of the spacious green, opposite Whipsnade's brick church, and at a sign for 'Tree Cathedral' turn right along a tarmac drive Ⓓ. Bear right to continue along a track and go through a gate into the grounds of Whipsnade Tree Cathedral, a variety of trees planted in the shape of a cathedral. This was created in 1931 by Edmund Blyth and was inspired by the building of Liverpool Cathedral, his experiences in the First World War and the loss of friends killed in that war. He bequeathed it to the National Trust.

The route continues along the left edge of the 'cathedral grounds' to a stile. Climb the stile, keep along the left-hand edge of a field to climb another stile and continue to a T-junction of paths. Turn right, following both Circular Route and Icknield Way signs, along a pleasantly tree- and hedge-lined path to reach the edge of the escarpment. Ahead is a magnificent view over the Vale of Aylesbury, with the line of the Chilterns stretching away to the left. The path bears right, but almost immediately turn left along a narrow path to a finger-post and turn right, in the Dunstable Downs direction, to a gate.

Go through the gate onto open downland for the superb finale to the walk. As you continue gently uphill across the slopes of the downs, there are extensive views over flat country to the left and a dramatic view ahead of the gently curving escarpment. The path leads directly back to the car park and visitor centre. ☐

RIGHT *The Dunstable Downs – a fine vantage point on the Chilterns escarpment*

County Gate, Brendon and Malmsmead Hill

This walk crosses part of what has become popularly known as 'Lorna Doone Country' because of its associations with R.D. Blackmore's well-known novel. It is an exceptionally fine walk beginning high up on the Devon-Somerset border, and it falls into two distinct parts. The first is along the side of the lovely, wooded valley of the East Lyn River; the second, in complete contrast, is a climb over bare and open moorland – Exmoor scenery at its very finest – before the descent into the Badgworthy valley at Malmsmead and final climb to County Gate. It is also a fairly strenuous walk, and because much of it is across open moorland with few landmarks it is best saved for a fine, clear day, when the extensive views can be fully appreciated.

Start	County Gate
Distance	9 miles (14.5 km)
Approximate time	5 hours
Parking	County Gate
Refreshments	Light refreshments at County Gate and Malmsmead, pub and tearooms at Brendon, pub at Rockford
Ordnance Survey maps	Landranger 180 (Barnstaple & Ilfracombe), Outdoor Leisure 9 (Exmoor), Pathfinder 1214, SS 64/74 (Lynton & Lynmouth)

One of the finest of Exmoor landscapes – the view from the start of the walk

County Gate is situated high up between the moors and the sea at the point where the main road between Porlock and Lynmouth crosses the Devon-Somerset border. From the car park take the path to the right, at a footpath sign to Brendon and Malmsmead, that contours along the edge of the steep-sided valley of Ashton Cleave, with superb views to the left of Malmsmead below, the Badgworthy valley beyond and rolling moors on the horizon. Follow this attractive path above the East Lyn River, descending slightly to go through a gate, and continue along the well-defined, red-waymarked route, curving right and left, crossing a footbridge over a small brook and bearing left. Climb a stile, descend a few steps and continue, passing through a gate. Brendon can be seen ahead nestling in its sheltered valley as the path continues through two more gates and then again descends, turning sharp left over a stile and onto a road **Ⓐ**. Bear left along the road into Brendon.

Do not turn left over the bridge but keep ahead for 100 yards (91 m) along the road signposted to Lynton and Porlock, by the East Lyn, and just before it bends to the right bear left, at a public footpath sign to Rockford and Watersmeet, along a riverside path, passing to the right of the telephone exchange. The path passes through a gate, crosses a field and goes through another gate by a house. For the next ¾ mile (1.25 km) keep beside or above the East Lyn along the edge of steep woodland to the right – a beautiful stretch of the route. Shortly after going through a gate turn left over the footbridge at Rockford **Ⓑ** and turn left along the road, retracing your route but on the opposite side of the river, for ¼ mile (0.5 km). Opposite a house on the left, and at a public footpath sign to Brendon Common, turn right onto a narrow path **Ⓒ** that heads very steeply uphill through thick woodland, by the right-hand side of a stream. Continue to a footpath sign and onto a road.

Turn left, following directions to 'Brendon Common via Shilstone', for about 300 yards (274 m). Where the road bends sharply to the left **D** go up some steps, climb a red-waymarked stile – the public footpath sign here to 'Brendon Common via Shilstone Hill' is difficult to see in the hedge – and continue uphill along the right-hand edge of a field, by a hedge-bank and trees on the right. At the top end of the field bear right through a hedge gap, head straight across to Shilstone Farm, go through a metal gate to walk through the middle of the farm buildings and on through another metal gate. Keep ahead for a few yards and then turn right downhill to cross a stream. Head up the other side, bearing left and continuing by a hedge-bank and wire fence on the right. Where the hedge-bank curves right keep ahead across the heathery moorland of Shilstone Hill – the route is defined by a line of red-topped posts – to the triangulation pillar at the summit (1,328 feet (405 m)). From here the views are magnificent, especially ahead over Brendon Common. Continue past a cairn, dropping gently to the road ahead at Dry Bridge **E**, which is situated in some of the most extensive and loneliest moorland landscape that Exmoor can offer.

Here bear left onto a broad track that curves left, bear left again on meeting another track and continue along it in a north-easterly direction across the heather, with superb views all around over the wild, treeless moorland. Keep along this track for the next 2 miles (3.25 km), following the direction of a public bridleway sign to Doone Valley at the first path junction, and at the second footpath sign continuing in the direction of Malmsmead. Keep ahead at the next junction of tracks – signposted to Malmsmead and Brendon – drop down over a ford and continue, still following signs to Malmsmead and Brendon, over Malmsmead Hill to reach a road **F**. Turn right along it for nearly 1 mile (1.5 km), heading downhill towards Malmsmead, with a glorious view of

the Badgworthy valley ahead, then turn sharp left into the hamlet.

Turn right over the bridge by Lorna Doone Farm and continue along the road, turning left at a footpath sign to Ashton, County Gate and Oare **G**. Go through a metal gate, walk down a farm track,

through a gate, across a footbridge over Oare Water and continue up to a stile and footpath sign. Here turn left – the route is signposted to County Gate – along a path that climbs steeply above the valley (the stream becomes the East Lyn River after the confluence of Oare Water and

Badgworthy Water), with more superb views to the left over the valley, Malmsmead and the moors. After an unremitting climb between gorse and bracken, the path levels off and continues by a wire fence on the right, passing through a gate to return to County Gate. □

SCALE 1 : 25 000 or 2½ INCHES to 1 MILE

Devil's Dyke

Starting from one of southern England's finest viewpoints, the rest of this walk continues in the same vein. The climb back to the ridge at the end is an exhilarating finale to a route which combines the best features of downland- and field-walking, as well as visiting two charming villages.

Start	Devil's Dyke Hotel
Distance	3½ miles (5.5 km)
Approximate time	2½ hours
Parking	Devil's Dyke Hotel
Refreshments	Pubs at start, Poynings and Fulking
Ordnance Survey maps	Landranger 198 (Brighton & The Downs), Pathfinder 1288, TQ 21/31 (Burgess Hill)

On a fine day you may have to arrive early to find a place in the car park at the Devil's Dyke Hotel. The spectacular view makes this a popular venue, and its airiness attracts kite-flyers. With your back to the hotel, turn right and walk past the large stone memorial seat (which dates from 1928 when the Dyke estate was given to the nation), continuing in a north-easterly direction along the crest of the ridge. Ignore a stile on the left.

When the path comes to another stile climb it and descend to another path below **A** which follows a ledge. Turn left onto

this bridleway and follow it northwards to a beautiful wood, where it begins to descend more steeply and can become very muddy after wet weather. The subsequent level path into Poynings can also be muddy. When this path reaches the main street turn right if you wish to visit the pub, otherwise turn left and pass the post office. On the apex of the following bend look for a footpath sign on the right pointing into a short lane **B**. This leads to a gate, which opens into a long meadow. Go ahead on a path and at the far end of the meadow go through a gate to join a track.

Turn left over a stile **C** onto an attractive path running along the bank of a stream that flows through two ponds. After these cross the stream by a bridge and then make for another stile on the far side of a meadow. A second meadow follows, crossed by a sunken field path. Continue straight across the next large field – this is enjoyable walking with a fine view of the Devil's Dyke ridge to the left and rolling countryside ahead and to the right. Cross the small field that follows to reach a lane **D**

Turn right and follow the lane for 250 yards (228 m) before turning left immediately after a small bridge **E**. Go over the stile by the side of a concrete drive signposted 'Brookside'. A short, rather overgrown stretch leads to a stile into a field. Here the going is easier, with the sound of running water on the left. Climb the stile leading out of the field, then cross a bridge and another stile, and walk 50 yards (46 m) by a stream to find a bridge over it on the left. Cross this and follow a field path heading south. The path runs along the right-hand side of a succession of fields, crossing a farm track at one point. Towards the end of the field nearest the houses turn right and climb a stile almost hidden in the undergrowth.

Keep to the edge of the field for about 50 yards (46 m), turn left through a gap and then cross the next field diagonally, making for the end of the brick wall

Down to the woods from Devil's Dyke

belonging to the white house at the top. A stile here leads to a paddock: keep to the left side of this to reach Fulking.

Turn right down the lane and immediately before the pub take a bridleway on the left **F**. After 50 yards (46 m) look for steps up the bank on the right, from which a footpath leads off. This footpath provides a demanding climb up the Fulking escarpment before the open downland is reached. Keep straight on where five footpaths cross **G** and after this the Devil's Dyke Hotel comes into sight ahead.

RIGHT *Looking over the Weald from the South Downs viewpoint of Devil's Dyke*

Cliffs and beaches

Britain's long and immensely varied coastline provides an unusually wide range of walking opportunities, from easy saunters along low cliffs or by marshes and sandy beaches, to lengthy and demanding walks in remote and rugged terrain.

The attractions of coastal walking are many. Few can fail to be fascinated by the sea in its many changing moods, the scenery is nearly always dramatic, and many coast walks can be enjoyed as part of a family holiday while staying in a nearby seaside resort. Route finding is straightforward – it is virtually impossible to lose your way – and except on particularly remote stretches a coastal path can usually be combined with inland paths to create a satisfying circular route. One of the following walks, along the Pembrokeshire coast path around the peninsula's heavily indented coastline, hardly leaves the sea at all.

Much of the tremendous variety of Britain's coast is featured in the selection here: from the low cliffs on the Norfolk and North Yorkshire coasts and the castle-strewn coast of Northumberland to the spectacular chalk cliffs of the Seven Sisters in Sussex and the more rugged coastlines of Cornwall and South Wales.

Remember that walking on high and exposed cliffs in bad weather, especially gale-force winds, should not be undertaken lightly and that some cliff walks, with their constant 'ups and downs', can be more tiring than a long mountain climb or moorland hike. Simply chose a walk that suits both you and the weather conditions best, take your time and enjoy some of the most visually exciting walking that this country can offer.

FLORA AND FAUNA

Pink thrift borders clifftop paths in spring and clumps of white sea campion grow from fissures in the rocks below. Herring gulls nest here and there on the cliffs along which fulmar petrels patrol continuously, up and down, on stiff outstretched wings.

On the beach, yellow horned-poppies and mats of wall pepper are in flower on shingle banks where oystercatchers and ringed plovers hide clutches of eggs amongst the pebbles. Meanwhile, common terns *(above)* dive for fish offshore.

Zennor to St Ives by the Tinners' Way

*This is a fine walk along one of the most spectacular parts of the Cornish coast. The inland section is hardly less enjoyable, a clearly marked path linking farmsteads, each about ½ mile (0.75 km) apart. Many of the small fields and their stone hedges date from prehistoric times. Although some of the inland path has signs showing it is part of the Tinners' Way, it is known locally as the Coffin Path. The coastal path definitely lives up to its name, often dipping down almost to the shoreline before soaring up again to the clifftop. The walk can be shortened, if wished, after point **A** below.*

Start	Zennor
Distance	8½ miles (13.5 km). Shorter version 5 miles (8 km)
Approximate time	4½ hours (2½ hours for shorter version)
Parking	Car park at Zennor
Refreshments	Pub at Zennor
Ordnance Survey maps	Landranger 203 (Land's End), Pathfinder 1364, SW 33/43 (St Ives & Penzance)

Either at the start or finish of the walk, be sure to visit the church at Zennor. Its most famous feature is the pew-end depicting the Zennor mermaid. There is also a bygones museum here. D.H. Lawrence used to drink at the Tinner's Arms during the First World War, when he was living in a cottage nearby writing *Women in Love*. He was eventually forced to leave the village with his German wife because the locals suspected them of being spies.

The path starts at the western end of the churchyard. There is a gate between the wall of the churchyard and a barn which leads to a meadow with a path alongside

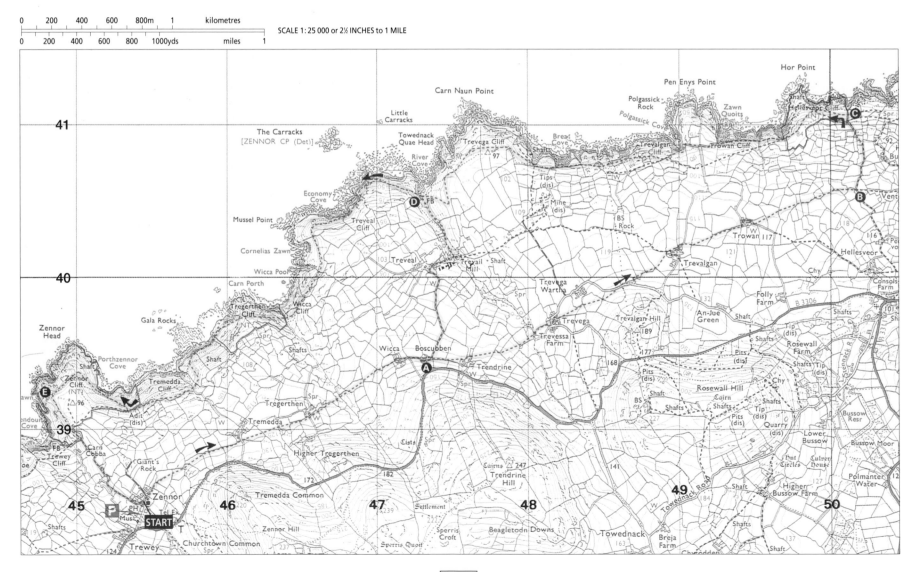

Gurnard's Head can be seen in the distance in this photograph taken from Zennor Head. This walk provides a superb succession of scenes such as this

the wall on the left. It is a very easy path to follow, as it goes in a more-or-less straight line over a series of stone stiles and cattle-grids which are easily seen ahead. If in doubt head for the next farmstead. From Tremedda follow the electricity lines and at Tregerthen go to the right of the farm to a narrow enclosed path which still follows the electricity line quite closely. After this point the stiles are clearly marked by striped posts.

Pass through the farmyard at Wicca and follow the farm track to Boscubben **A**. After the farm take the track to the left.

Those wishing to do only the shorter version of the walk can follow this track towards the coastal path, rejoining the main route there **D**.

After about 50 yards (46 m) the main route branches off the track to the right,

over a stone stile marked by a striped pole. At Trendrine there is a Tinners' Way route-mark. Pass through the farmyard with the house on the right, then head for the next house, Trevessa, across the field. At Trevessa turn left onto the lane and then immediately right by Little Trevega. Head for a modern-looking house at the top through the next long meadow and go to the right of it, following electricity wires to find the next waymark. Climb the stile into the lane, turn right, and after 200 yards (183 m) turn left, following Tinners' Way signs. Trevalgan is the next farm.

The path passes to the left of the farm, and the next farmstead, Trowan, is in a straight line ahead. Carry straight on from here too, still following the clearly marked path, until it arrives at a farm track which is a footpath crossroads **B**. If you wish to visit St Ives go straight on – it is about

half-an-hour's walk but be warned that it involves a steep climb back to the coastal footpath which is joined at the western end of Porthmeor Beach. Our route, omitting St Ives, turns left along the track to join the coastal footpath on Hellesveor Cliff **C**. Turn westwards (to the left) after admiring the view eastwards across St Ives Bay to Godrevy lighthouse and beyond.

There is an even better view back from the next headland – Pen Enys – where planks are laid so that the worst of the mud at the valley bottom is avoided. The spot-height marked at the triangulation pillar on Trevega Cliff is 300 feet (91 m). After this the view opens up westwards to Pendeen lighthouse. Strangely there is no point where you can get views of a lighthouse in each direction: Godrevy to the east and Pendeen to the west. Just beyond River

Cove a path joins from Treveal: this is the shorter, alternative route **D**.

Continue along the coastal path and from the next headland, Mussel Point, the view to Zennor and Gurnard's headlands is even better than before. After Tregerthen this is a true coastal path – one moment plunging to the shoreline, the next high up on the cliffs above, and usually twisting through a scattering of enormous boulders. You may think that you have reached Zennor Head when you have climbed up to the rock tower that overlooks Porthzennor Cove, but this is a false summit. You have to walk to the next tor **E**, which has a plaque on it, to find the true Zennor Head. The views from both prominences are spectacular.

The path back to the village follows the valley, soon joining a lane which leads to the church and the Tinner's Arms. ☐

Wooltack Point and Marloes

A combination of dramatic cliff scenery, sandy beaches, superb views and relatively flat, easy walking make for the perfect coastal walk. The narrow Marloes peninsula forms the southern arm of St Bride's Bay and the prominent headland of Wooltack Point is at the tip of it. Apart from crossing the neck of the peninsula near Marloes village, the walk keeps by the sea all the while, following the coast round.

Start	Martin's Haven
Distance	7 miles (11.25 km)
Approximate time	4 hours
Parking	National Trust car park at Martin's Haven
Refreshments	Pubs at Marloes
Ordnance Survey maps	Landranger 157 (St David's & Haverfordwest), Pathfinder 1102, SM 70 (Skomer Island)

Gateholm Island, near Marloes

At the far end of the car park walk along a lane to where it bears right to the jetty at Martin's Haven by some stone gateposts. The posts are in a wall built to enclose a deer park that it was planned to establish here in the eighteenth century, but the plan never materialised. Pass between the posts, climb a stile and keep ahead up steps to do a circuit of this proposed deer park, passing a coastguard lookout hut and continuing to Wooltack Point **A**, the rocky headland at the western tip of the Marloes peninsula. This is a magnificent viewpoint: to the right you look across St Bride's Bay to St David's Head, and to the left and ahead are the offshore islands of Skokholm and Skomer, both important sanctuaries for birds and grey seals.

From Wooltack Point turn sharply left along the cliffs, following a series of waymarks and a line of yellow-topped posts to reach a stile just below the starting point **B**. Climb it and continue along the rugged south coast of the peninsula, with fine views to the right of Skokholm Island, passing by the rocky, flat-topped Gateholm Island, and later keeping above the fine, flat, long beach of Marloes Sands.

Descend some steps into a steep-sided valley and at the bottom turn left, leaving the coast path **C**, to head up a stony track. This bends sharply to the left, later curves right and continues to a lane **D**. Turn right along it for nearly ½ mile (0.75 km) and just after passing a farm on the right turn left **E** over a stile, at a public footpath sign, and walk along the right-hand edge of a field, by a hedge-bank and wire fence on the right. Climb a stile and keep ahead, climbing another stile onto a road. To visit the village of Marloes, which has pubs, a church and a clock tower, turn right, but the route continues to the left along the road as far as a public footpath sign, where you turn right over a stile **F**.

Walk along the right-hand edge of a field towards the sea and at the bottom end follow the direction of a public footpath sign to the left to continue along a narrow path. At a fork take the left-hand path, shortly rejoining the coast path **G** and follow it for the next 2 miles (3.25 km), now along the north side of the peninsula but with the same combination of fairly easy walking and spectacular cliff scenery as before. On reaching the cove of Martin's Haven bear left and descend to a tarmac lane. Turn left along it to the stone gateposts bordering the 'deer park' and turn left again to return to the car park. □

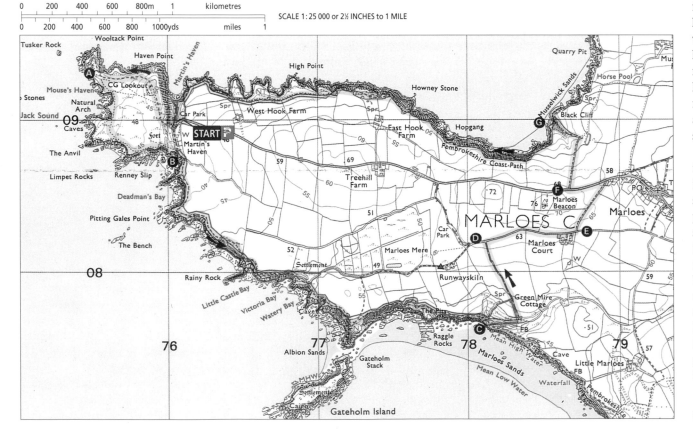

SCALE 1: 25 000 or 2½ INCHES to 1 MILE

RIGHT *The curving beach of Marloes Sands*

Robin Hood's Bay and Ravenscar

The track of the disused Whitby–Scarborough Railway makes possible a splendid circular coastal walk linking Robin Hood's Bay and Ravenscar. On the first part of the walk, the inland section, the track provides a quick route to Ravenscar, a superb vantage point from where the view over the bay is magnificent. The return route to Robin Hood's Bay keeps to the coastal path along a spectacular section of the North Yorkshire coast. The first half of the walk is obviously flat and easy; the second half is rather more energetic.

Start	Robin Hood's Bay
Distance	9 miles (14.5 km)
Approximate time	4½ hours
Parking	Robin Hood's Bay
Refreshments	Pubs and cafés at Robin Hood's Bay, hotel at Ravenscar
Ordnance Survey maps	Landranger 94 (Whitby), Outdoor Leisure 27 (North York Moors – Eastern area)

The last part of the walk spread out ahead – the splendid sweep of Robin Hood's Bay seen from Ravenscar

A jumble of red-roofed cottages clustered together below steep cliffs, with narrow winding lanes, passages and stepped paths leading down to the sea, make up the enchanting fishing village of Robin Hood's Bay. Its previous remoteness and inaccessibility made it a notorious haunt for smugglers, and like Staithes and other places along this coast, parts of the village have in the past been swept away by storms and had to be rebuilt. Its name comes from a tradition that at some time Robin Hood fled here to escape from his pursuers by boarding a fishing vessel, but as with all Robin Hood stories there is no factual basis for it. An added attraction of Robin Hood's Bay is that because of the narrow streets no cars are allowed; motorists have to park at one of two main car parks at the top of the village.

The walk begins at Station car park where you turn right past the former station buildings and follow a tarmac lane to a road. Turn right for about 100 yards (91 m) and where the road bends to the right turn left through a gate Ⓐ to join the track of the disused Whitby–Scarborough Railway, built in 1885, closed in 1965 but happily converted into a footpath. Keep along the pleasantly tree-lined track for 4½ miles (7.25 km) to Ravenscar, crossing several roads and passing under several bridges, sometimes going through deep wooded cuttings and at other times along embankments, with some fine views over gentle wooded hills to the right and over the coast to the left.

Where the track swings back towards the coast there is a particularly fine view over Robin Hood's Bay and the prominent headland of Ravenscar. Approaching Ravenscar, you can see the now-overgrown remains of disused alum quarries. After passing through some of these quarries, bear left to a T-junction of paths and turn right along a paved path up to the road Ⓑ, passing a National Trust information centre on the left. In the late nineteenth century there were grandiose plans to develop Ravenscar as a major resort, but they came to nothing, one of the reasons being the instability of the rocks in the area. The most notable building is the Raven Hall Hotel on the headland, built in the eighteenth century (and once visited by George III) and enlarged in the nineteenth century. It occupies the site of a Roman signal station.

On reaching the road immediately turn left down a broad track, signposted 'To the shore', to the left of the entrance to the Raven Hall Hotel. From this track there is the finest view of the walk, across the broad sweep of Robin Hood's Bay to the buildings of the village huddled together on the far side. Pass below the hotel walls to the right and follow the path as it curves sharply to the left at a finger-post **C**, following directions to Robin Hood's Bay. This part of the walk can be quite hazardous at times as it crosses the Raven Hall golf course. Shortly afterwards the path bends to the right to run parallel to the coast, and soon after descending into a wooded area it joins the Cleveland Way coming in from the left.

Keep along the Cleveland Way, a well-waymarked route with plenty of Cleveland Way signs which crosses several stiles and footbridges and has the magnificent view over the bay ahead all the while. Nearing Robin Hood's Bay the path meets a lane **D**; turn right along it for a few yards and then continue downhill along a paved path through a wooded dell, over a footbridge at the bottom by a small shingle beach, and steeply up steps on the other side onto the clifftop. Now the path hugs the edge of the cliffs before descending steeply into Boggle Hole **E**.

The coast path north of Boggle Hole has been lost due to coastal erosion. A new path may be made along the clifftop, and if so will be waymarked. Otherwise, follow the waymarked diversion route by turning left up a steep tarmac road. At the car park at the top turn right onto another tarmac road, pass to the right of South House Farm and drop steeply down to Mill

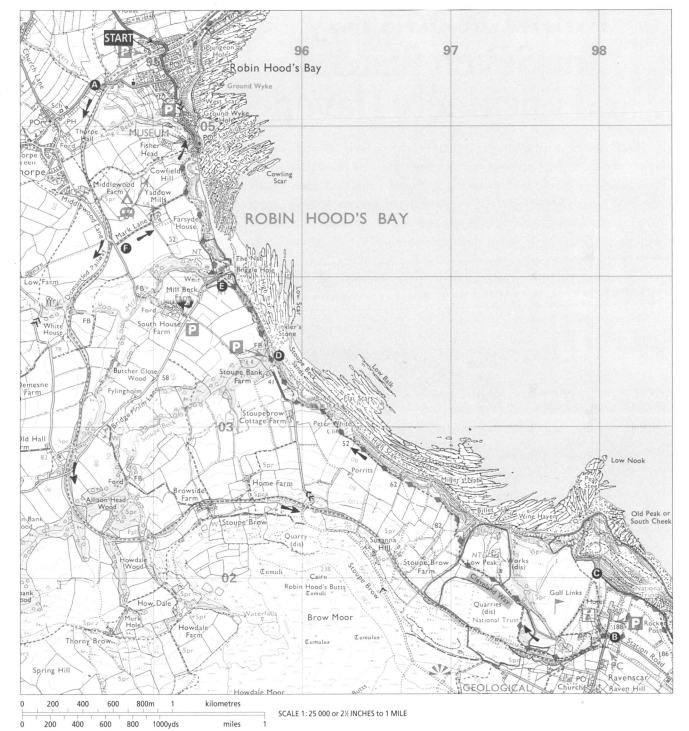

Beck. Cross the footbridge and continue up the road until a junction on the right immediately before the old railway track **F**. Turn right into Mark Lane and follow it as far as Farsyde House, then follow the waymarked path to the left to rejoin the clifftop path. Turn left onto it and there is a lovely view of the picturesque village huddled below. Drop down through trees into Robin Hood's Bay and walk through its narrow streets and alleys steeply uphill back to Station car park.

Friston Forest, the Seven Sisters and Cuckmere Haven

Forest, downs, coast and river combine to create a most satisfying and superbly varied walk. A pleasant ramble along wide, green tracks through the woodlands of Friston Forest is followed by a walk across open downland to reach the coast. Then comes the scenic highlight and most strenuous part of the route: a series of quite steep climbs over four of the Seven Sisters, the succession of chalk cliffs that lie just to the west of Beachy Head and one of the most spectacular stretches of coastline in England. After Cuckmere Haven a gentle stroll by the meandering River Cuckmere is a relaxing finale.

Start	Seven Sisters Country Park car park at Exceat
Distance	6½ miles (10.5 km)
Approximate time	3½ hours
Parking	Exceat
Refreshments	Farm café at Exceat
Ordnance Survey maps	Landranger 199 (Eastbourne & Hastings), Pathfinder 1324, TV 49/59/69 (Eastbourne & Seaford)

Nowadays Exceat is little more than a name on a map and a few farm buildings by a bridge over the River Cuckmere; the village was abandoned after the Black Death and a series of French raids. Its remains and the site of the church lie buried under fields. An eighteenth-century converted barn serves as a visitor centre for the Seven Sisters Country Park, which covers the area of downland, river, estuary and coast to the south. Next door to this is a fascinating 'Living World' exhibition, containing many rare insects.

Turn right out of the car park along the main road and take the first track on the left, at a South Downs Way sign. Climb a stile, bear slightly right and head uphill across a field to go through a gate, immediately climbing a stone stile in a wall to enter Friston Forest, a delightful area of mixed woodland managed by the Forestry Commission. Take the path signposted to Westdean through the trees, descending via a long flight of steps into the sleepy and unspoilt village. Turn right along a lane **Ⓐ**, at a public bridleway sign to Friston and Jevington. Just before reaching a Friston Forest sign, a short detour to the left brings you to the small, plain church with the short tower and spire typical of Sussex.

Keep ahead along the lane, heading uphill into woodland again where the tarmac lane becomes a forest track. This broad track is followed through the forest for nearly 1½ miles (2.5 km). At a fork take the right-hand uphill track in the Friston direction, and later, where the roughly made-up forest track veers left, go ahead on a grassy path. Descend to cross a track, continue uphill again, keeping along the right-hand edge of an area of open grassland, and finally head downhill to pass beside a barrier onto a tarmac drive **Ⓑ**.

Turn left, and where the drive bends right keep ahead along a track to a footpath sign just in front of a barrier. Turn right, in the Friston direction, along a path that runs parallel to the tarmac drive on the right. At a yellow-waymarked public footpath sign turn right, following directions to Friston and East Dean, up steps and through a gate.

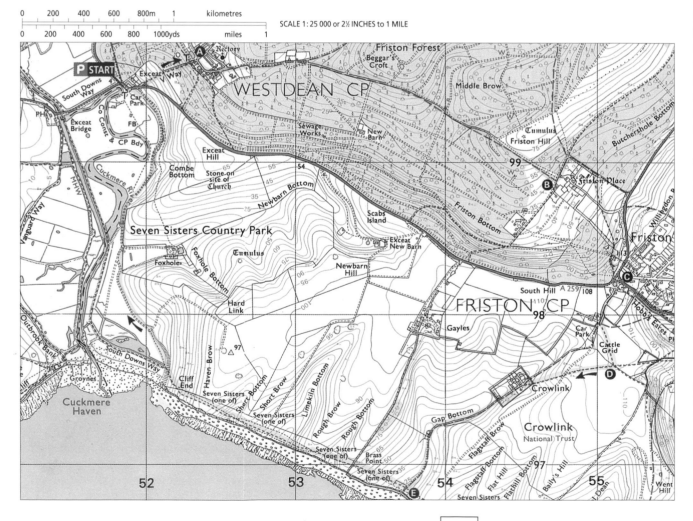

Keep straight ahead across a field, go through a gate on the far side and descend steps to a tarmac drive. Cross it, bear slightly left to climb the stile opposite and continue diagonally and slightly uphill across a field to another stile in the far corner. Climb it and follow a path through woodland, finally climbing a third stile and keeping ahead to meet the main road again at a junction **C**.

Cross the road and take the tarmac track opposite (signposted 'Crowlink, no through road'), passing between a lily pond on the right and Friston's small, attractive church on the left. The tarmac track soon becomes a rough track. Just before entering the National Trust's Crowlink car park, turn

left through a gate and then turn half-right diagonally across a field. Go through a gate and bear right along a rather indistinct path **D**, keeping in a straight line diagonally across the field. Although the numerous paths across this National Trust property may appear confusing, there is no problem; once you reach the brow of a hill, simply make for the prominent group of farm buildings seen below. Look out for a stile in a wire fence, climb it and continue downhill to pass through a hedge gap onto a track.

Turn left along the track, passing to the left of the farm buildings, go through a gate and walk through the dry valley of Gap Bottom, keeping by a wire fence and

hedge on the right. Continue along a wide, smooth, grassy path which winds through the shallow valley bottom to the edge of the cliffs **E**

Turn right onto the South Downs Way to Cuckmere Haven, a route that climbs over four of the series of chalk cliffs known as the Seven Sisters. There are some steep 'ups and downs' on this section but the superb cliff scenery and the magnificent, extensive views more than compensate for the effort expended. Over the last brow you look down on Cuckmere Haven, the beautiful and unspoilt estuary of the Cuckmere, with its shingle beach, lagoons and meandering river, and beyond that to Seaford Head.

Descend steeply towards the beach and just before the final, very steep descent, turn right over a stile and continue along the side of the valley above the river. Head gently downhill along a pleasant, grassy path, go through a gate and bear right along a track. At a T-junction of tracks bear right again, go through a gate and continue along a concrete track to the right of the marshes, lagoons and great meanders of the Cuckmere, among the finest examples of river meanders in Britain. In 1846 this section of the river was straightened and canalised to reduce flooding. As you near Exceat, bear left onto a grassy track which leads directly back to the car park. □

The spectacular chalk cliffs of the Seven Sisters, where the South Downs meet the sea, offer exhilarating walking on the Sussex coast

Sheringham Park and Pretty Corner

The beautiful woodland of Sheringham Park is at its best in springtime and early summer when the rhododendrons are in bloom. Many of these are rare varieties specially collected from the Himalayas in the mid nineteenth century for the owner of Sheringham Hall, Mr Upcher. The woods also have an abundance of bluebells and daffodils. After this wonderful start the route maintains interest through its variety. A fine walk along high (for Norfolk) clifftops leads to Sheringham promenade, and there is an opportunity to look at the Edwardian resort. A climb to the vantage point of Beeston Hill marks the start of the second part of the route, which returns to the park through woodland and by quiet lanes.

Start	Sheringham Park (entrance at junction of A148 and B1157, Upper Sheringham)
Distance	11½ miles (18·5 km)
Approximate time	5 hours
Parking	National Trust car park, Sheringham Park
Refreshments	Pubs and cafés at Sheringham, pub at Upper Sheringham
Ordnance Survey maps	Landranger 133 (North East Norfolk), Pathfinder 820, TG 04/14 (Sheringham & Blakeney)

Start by following a blue- and red-waymarked route, entering woodland to the left of the car park. A field is on the left and the path descends steeply into a dell with banks of rhododendrons. The trees have suffered some storm damage and there has been considerable replanting. The blue route goes off to the right by a tall oak and a V-shaped beech, but we follow the red arrows and pass some chestnuts of a wonderful size. After a pond the path climbs to a vantage point with more rhododendrons. The prospect here is being restored to the one sketched by Humphry Repton, the designer of the park, in his Red Book.

Join the drive to Sheringham Hall here – dogs should be on leads from this point through the parkland – but turn left before the hall to reach a gate giving onto a field-edge track. This runs by Oak Wood; a signposted path Ⓐ on the right into the wood leads up to the Gazebo – the path must be one of the steepest in the county. The Gazebo's original wooden structure was replaced in 1988 by the present steel tower, which is a magnificent viewpoint for coastline and park.

Returning to the track from the Gazebo, turn right to reach the road. Cross this to a path which runs parallel to the road along another field edge and joins a track going seawards. Note the pebble-built barn on the left before the railway bridge over the North Norfolk Railway, a preserved section of the old Midland & Great Northern. On the cliff edge turn right onto the Norfolk Coast Path Ⓑ.

The cliffs are very unstable, so keep well away from the edge. At a height of 165 feet (50 m) or so they are among the highest in Norfolk. National Trust land is left when the path reaches the golf-course. Keep to the coast path, which dips and then climbs to an old coastguard lookout before it reaches Sheringham promenade. There is an opportunity to walk on the shore, but since the beach is made up of small, round pebbles progress will be slow, and later on large boulders are

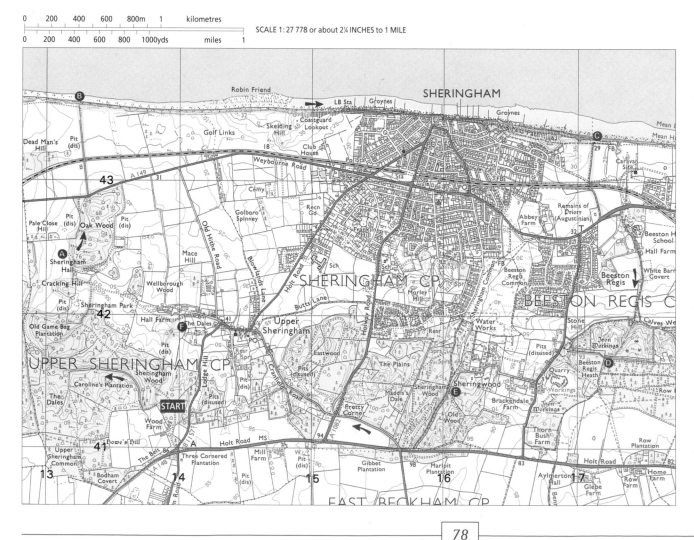

Sheringham is a delightful resort which retains much of its early Edwardian character. Here it is seen from the clifftop footpath to the west of the town

heaped up as a sea defence. Remain on the upper promenade until, by a children's playground, steps lead down to the lower promenade. Keep on this, past the centre of the resort, to a toilet block faced with bright yellow tiles. Climb up the steps here to a concrete drive, and bear left off this at a signpost to Beeston Hill, at a putting green **Ⓒ**.

The path climbs to the triangulation point, a viewpoint rivalling the Gazebo earlier in the walk. From here the coast path descends to a caravan park, with a view of the lovely Beeston church. Turn right at the boundary fence to cross the railway and reach the road. Turn left for about 20 yards (18 m) and then cross to an old section of the main road, which leads

to another caravan site. Turn right at a post-box onto a track which leads past Beeston Hall School. Hall Farm has walls made of seashore pebbles, skilfully laid. The track climbs towards woods.

Leave the Norfolk Coast Path when the woods are reached, and take the path straight ahead into them. This is a bridleway well used by horse-riders. Turn right when this path reaches a fence **Ⓓ** and keep this on the left. This is level walking on a heathy ridge with young trees on each side. The path soon descends steeply to reach a lane.

Turn left, and after the Carter concrete works on the left turn right onto the track to Sheringwood. This driveway is twisty. Bear right and then fork left, ignoring

signs to Owls Oak, Breckland and Sandywood. Bear left past Robin Hill to pass Bramble Cottage and so reach the track into the woods, with a boundary fence on the left.

Follow it and soon fork right, dropping to a path at the bottom of the dell, and turn left onto this following a yellow, white and blue waymark. When this path meets with another path crossing it **Ⓔ** go directly over to a very straight track with banks on either side. This climbs, steeply at the end, to the main road. Turn right, and then right again at the crossroads onto the lane leading to Pretty Corner.

This is a famous beauty spot, and easy access to the acres of woodland and heath makes it very popular. Cross another road

beyond the car park and walk down Cranfield Road into Upper Sheringham. Pass the post office, pub and church, all on the left, and where the Holt road goes off to the left keep on the Weybourne road for a few yards before continuing straight on into a cul-de-sac leading to a gate into Sheringham Park.

About 200 yards (183 m) beyond the gate turn to the left off the drive **Ⓕ**, following a red waymark to the Temple. This was erected by Mr Upcher in 1975. Follow the orange and red waymark on its far side to descend the hill and reach a stile leading out of the park into woods. A steep climb follows to reach the other drive. Cross this and follow red, blue and orange waymarks to reach the car park. □

Craster and Dunstanburgh Castle

The trouble with really excellent short walks is that they become overcrowded, so choose your time for this one carefully. There are seldom crowds about early in the morning when the sea-light on the castle can be magical – as can that of late evening. The drawback to these times is that the opening time for the castle is 10 am and it is closed in the evening.

Start	Craster
Distance	4½ miles (7.25 km)
Approximate time	2½ hours
Parking	National Trust car park at Craster
Refreshments	Pubs and seasonal café at Craster
Ordnance Survey maps	Landrangers 75 (Berwick-upon-Tweed) and 81 (Alnwick & Morpeth), Pathfinder 477, NU 21/22 (Embleton & Alnmouth)

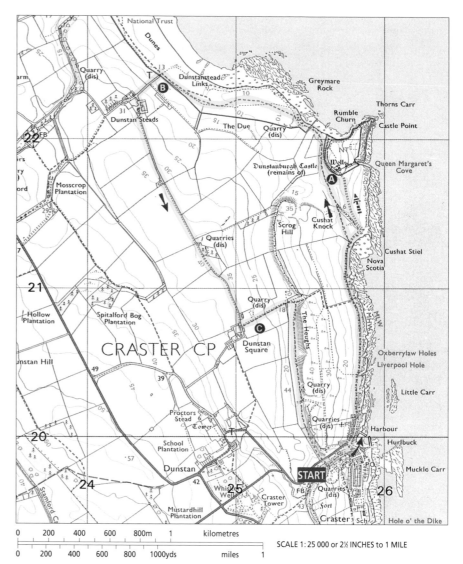

The National Trust car park at Craster occupies the old quarry, which like most of the village was owned by the family which gave the place its name. The family lived in Craster for more than seven centuries. Whinstone produced by the quarry was sent to London and other great cities where it was used as kerbstones.

A path leads from the quarry to the harbour; turn northwards from here after taking in the charm of the small fishing village, famous for its delicious oak-smoked kippers. A few picturesque cobles, the distinctive craft of Northumbrian

Craster harbour

fishermen, usually rest in the harbour; once it was full of them. Craster harbour was built in 1906 by the family as a monument to Captain Craster who was killed during the British military expedition to Tibet in 1904.

The walk to the castle is on springy turf, with a platform of dolerite on the seaward side providing countless rock pools which children love to explore, discovering hermit crabs, anemones and periwinkles. This rock is volcanic in origin, intruded between other strata to form the distinctive 'sill' which at its seaward end makes a dramatic, and very secure, site for the castle **A**. The path divides at the approach to the castle: take the right fork if you wish to visit it; otherwise take the left fork through the ditch which once formed the castle's harbour and was used by the fleet of Henry VIII in 1514.

Walking beneath the walls of the stronghold it is easy to appreciate the difficulties faced by those besieging it. Dunstanburgh dates from 1314 and is by far the largest castle in Northumberland, covering eleven acres (4½ ha). The

precipitous dolerite crag forms the perfect defence on the two seaward sides, and to the west. Only to the south does the site lie open, and here the enormous gatehouse with its flanking towers defied attackers. During the Wars of the Roses it was twice besieged by the Earl of Warwick and was surrendered to him on each occasion. Subsequently it was left open to the elements, and these turned it into the picturesque ruin that we see today. It is hardly surprising that Dunstanburgh has a ghost, a wandering knight named Sir Guy, said to bewail his failure to free a captive maiden, whose

ghost appears on the ramparts on wild nights as a white lady.

The footpath leads northwards beneath the forbidding walls to reach the sea at the south end of Embleton Bay. The seabirds here are mostly kittiwakes which nest on the rocky ledges of Gull Crag. There follows a pleasant switchback walk along the crest of the sand-dunes, with a golf-course on the left. Note the fantastic swirl of lava on the shore at the beginning of this section just beyond the gate to Dunstanburgh Stead Links.

The route turns inland on the slatted track **B** which leads to the lane to

The ruined bastions of Dunstanburgh Castle are an early highlight of this walk. Built early in the fourteenth century, the castle was abandoned two centuries later

Dunstan Steads. At the farm turn left again, following the direction of the bridleway sign to Dunstan Square. From the concrete track through fields and meadows there are good views of the castle to the left, and of the long sill. Before the concept of landscape conservation took hold much material was quarried from the sill for roadstone. On the right is an endless view of farmland. Trees screen the brickwork of an old lime-kiln, which before the advent of artificial fertilisers was vital for cultivation. At Dunstan Square **C** turn left to the Heughs, the local name for the volcanic ridge. Then turn right to walk southwards in its shelter, welcome when the east wind is blowing. The path is broad at first but becomes narrow after a kissing-gate. It emerges in Craster directly opposite the car park. ☐

Hills and mountains

For many walkers Britain's hills and mountains are the greatest lure of all, offering the most satisfying and spectacular of all walking experiences.

The usual definition of a mountain is a hill over 2,000 feet (610 m) high and almost all of these, apart from a few in the Pennines and Dartmoor, are concentrated in Wales, Cumbria and Scotland. Compared with mountains in the rest of the world British mountains are low, but this in no way detracts from their great beauty or ruggedness. Scenic grandeur does not depend on statistics, as the two mountain walks chosen here – one in the Lake District and the other in the Brecon Beacons – strikingly illustrate.

Although people may have to travel long distances to walk in mountain regions, almost everybody lives within easy reach of hills; in fact probably the majority of walking done in this country is hill walking. It can offer views and landscapes as impressive as many mountain walks without some of the potential dangers, and can be done by those who might not feel confident or fit enough to tackle the more demanding and strenuous walks.

Hill walks can be in a landscape largely dominated by higher peaks, as in the walk in Perthshire in the following selection, or where the hills are the main feature of a traditionally lowland landscape, as with the walks in the Cotswolds and the Malverns. The latter, which rise almost sheer from the Severn plain, resemble a mountain range despite having a maximum height of only 1,395 feet (425 m).

FLORA AND FAUNA

In earlier times most hillside slopes were wooded. Now, due to human activities, the majority are covered with grass or heather. Common species such as the meadow pipit may visit such terrain, but in the gullies and small valleys which scar the landscape there is more of interest.

Scraggy, weather-beaten rowans and thorn bushes grow from clefts in the rocks, and primroses *(above)* and rare ferns find refuge on the steep banks. Ring ouzels nest on ledges, and the more inaccessible places sometimes accommodate a buzzard.

● Birks of Aberfeldy

● Ashness Bridge, Watendlath and Bowder Stone

Great Malvern and the
Worcestershire Beacon
● ●
Fan y Big and ●   Broadway and
Taf Fechan Forest   Broadway Tower

Ashness Bridge, Watendlath and Bowder Stone

This is an exceptionally beautiful walk, which has three scenic highlights that will remain i::delibly in the memory. The first is the well-known viewpoint from Ashness Bridge over Derwent Water and Skiddaw. Next, from a wooded perch high above the valley, comes the dramatic Surprise View. Finally there is the magnificent view of the head of Borrowdale soon after leaving Watendlath. Lakeshore, woodland, a huge isolated boulder and an idyllic secluded hamlet make this an outstandingly varied walk. The terrain is good throughout and there are only two modest climbs.

Start	Kettlewell car park on eastern shore of Derwent Water
Distance	8½ miles (13.5 km)
Approximate time	5 hours
Parking	Kettlewell car park by lakeshore. Alternatively, use Watendlath road car park, where road to Watendlath branches off Borrowdale road, and start walk from there
Refreshments	Cafés at Watendlath and Grange
Ordnance Survey maps	Landrangers 89 (West Cumbria) and 90 (Penrith, Keswick & Ambleside), Outdoor Leisure 4 (The English Lakes – North Western area)

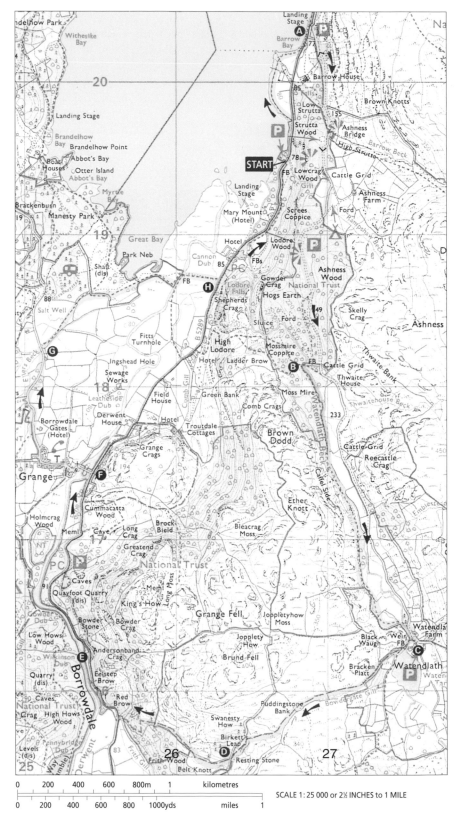

Start by turning right along the lakeshore and follow the curve of the shore around to rejoin the road by the Ashness landing-stage **A**. Go up some steps and take the narrow uphill lane straight ahead which is signposted to Ashness Bridge and Watendlath. Climb up to the old pack-horse bridge and look back to enjoy the magnificent panorama, a classic view which is a forerunner for the even more magnificent Surprise View, about ½ mile (0.75 km) further along the lane.

Surprise View is a precarious ledge on the edge of woodland, with a steep drop below, from where the view over Borrowdale, Derwent Water, Keswick and Bassenthwaite, with Skiddaw forming the dramatic backcloth, must surely be one of

the most outstanding in the country. From here follow a delightful path through the woods parallel to the lane. At a wall climb a ladder-stile, turn right over Watendlath Beck **B** and turn left to follow the beck, initially through woodland and later across meadows and below crags, for 1½ miles (2.5 km) into the idyllic, isolated hamlet of Watendlath. This is a lovely spot on the shores of Watendlath Tarn, nothing more than a small collection of farmhouses, but noted as the setting for the home of Judith Paris in the novels of Sir Hugh Walpole.

At Watendlath go through a gate **C**, bear right along the edge of the tarn, pass through another gate, and at a fork keep ahead along the uphill path at a public bridleway sign for Rosthwaite. The path climbs steadily, giving grand views behind over Watendlath. Where it levels off and starts to drop down into Borrowdale, there are magnificent views ahead of the white cottages of Rosthwaite, the lush green meadows below in the valley and the woods on the lower slopes of the fells; looking towards Honister, the head of the dale can be seen, framed by majestic and awe-inspiring peaks.

Descend by trees on the right, turn right through a gate at a footpath sign for Keswick and Bowder Stone **D**, and take a path which drops down to a gate, then passes into woods and continues to a road. Turn right along the road for ¼ mile (0.5 km) and by a gate turn right over a stile at a National Trust sign to Bowder Stone **E**. Follow a broad wooded path to the stone, an immense, isolated boulder left by retreating glaciers during the last ice age. It is estimated to weigh over 2,000 tons and a ladder on one side enables closer inspection and the opportunity to take in the view from the top.

Continue ahead to rejoin the Borrowdale road and keep along it, with good views of High Spy and Maiden Moor on the left, turning left over the old narrow bridge across the Derwent **F** into Grange. Walk through the village and along the lane for nearly ¾ mile (1.25 km), turning right through a gate at a public footpath sign to Lodore **G**. The path crosses low-lying, marshy grazing land, with convenient boardwalks in places, skirting Manesty Woods and bearing right across the foot of Derwent Water, with excellent views down the lake. Continue over the river and ahead to the Borrowdale road again **H**. Turn left along the road back to the car park; just past the Lodore Swiss Hotel you can walk along a pleasant National Trust path running parallel to the road through Strutta Wood, rejoining the road opposite the car park.

Rushing water, ancient bridge, woodland, lake and mountain – this classic view over Derwent Water and Skiddaw from Ashness Bridge shows the full grandeur of the Lake District

Great Malvern and the Worcestershire Beacon

Rising abruptly from the flat lands of the Vale of Severn in the east and the rolling hills of Herefordshire in the west, the Malvern Hills resemble a mountain range, despite attaining a maximum height of only 1,395 feet (425 m). This walk climbs from Great Malvern to the highest point, the Worcestershire Beacon, and continues along the ridge, with magnificent views all around, before descending and returning along paths that contour around the wooded lower slopes of the hills. This is Elgar country; the great composer was born and lived most of his life within sight of the Malverns, walked frequently on them and was undoubtedly inspired by them. The hills are honeycombed with paths and tracks, which can sometimes be a disadvantage – indeed it can prove difficult to keep to a precise route because of the proliferation of paths. But provided you do not go wandering on the hills in misty weather the various settlements that encircle them are in sight for most of the time; there are also a number of stone direction indicators, erected by the Malvern Hills Conservators, to show the way down. Interestingly the latter were formed in 1884, eleven years before the National Trust, and could thus claim to be the first organisation set up to conserve an area of great natural beauty.

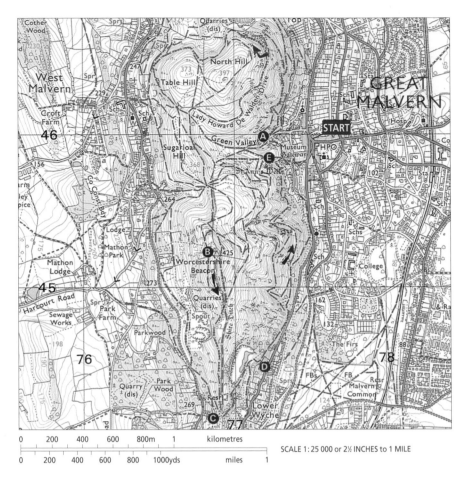

| 0 | 200 | 400 | 600 | 800m | 1 | | kilometres |
| 0 | 200 | 400 | 600 | 800 | 1000yds | | miles | 1 |

SCALE 1: 25 000 or 2½ INCHES to 1 MILE

Start	Great Malvern
Distance	5½ miles (8.75 km)
Approximate time	3 hours
Parking	Great Malvern
Refreshments	Pubs and cafés at Great Malvern, café at St Ann's Well
Ordnance Survey maps	Landranger 150 (Worcester & The Malverns), Pathfinder 1018, SO 64/74 (Great Malvern)

The Regency and Victorian hotels and villas that cover the slopes of the Malvern Hills reflect the heyday of Great Malvern as a popular spa and health resort. Much older is the grand priory church in the town centre, founded in 1085. The nave is Norman and the rest of the church, including the imposing central tower, is a fine example of the Perpendicular style of the fifteenth century.

Start at the meeting of roads in the centre of Great Malvern, just to the north of the priory, and walk along Belle Vue Terrace in the Worcester direction, turning left along St Ann's Road. This narrow road heads steeply uphill and later becomes a tarmac track which continues up through the steep-sided, tree-lined Happy Valley. Where the tarmac track swings sharply to the left at a junction of several tracks **A**, turn

sharp right, at a stone indicator to Ivy Scar Rock, and a few yards ahead bear right along a broad track which contours along the lower slopes of the wooded hills.

Keep on the main track all the while as it winds around, climbing gently to pass to the right of Ivy Scar Rock. A few yards beyond the wooden bench below the rock bear slightly left onto a narrower uphill path between gorse, scrub and bracken, following it around a series of zig-zag bends to reach a T-junction. Here turn right along a grand, broad, flat track – Lady Howard De Walden Drive. At a fork the drive continues along the left-hand uphill track; follow it as it curves first to the left around North Hill, giving fine views to the north, and later to both right and left around Table Hill. Now there are superb views westwards across the rolling country of Herefordshire.

At a fork just before a left-hand bend take the uphill track to the left which heads over Table Hill – the houses of West Malvern are below on the right – to reach a junction of tracks. Keep ahead until you join a broad, clear, stony track by a sharp bend and turn right to follow it towards the summit of the Worcestershire Beacon. At a crossroads keep ahead, and at a circular stone indicator where several alternative routes to the beacon are shown, it is probably easiest to keep along the main track. This curves upwards and finally turns sharp right to reach the triangulation pillar, sheltered picnic area and circular toposcope – the latter erected to commemorate Queen Victoria's diamond jubilee – on the 1,395-foot (425 m) summit. This is the highest point on the Malverns and a superb all-round viewpoint **B**.

From the summit continue along the magnificent ridge path, with grand views on both sides and a spectacular view of the Malverns stretching away in front, dipping up and down like a roller-coaster. Descend to join a tarmac track and follow it gently downhill to reach another circular stone indicator **C**. Turn sharp left in the direction of 'Quarry Walk and St Ann's Well via Earnslaw' along a dclightful wooded track. At a fork take the left-hand, broader grassy track that heads gently uphill again to pass above a huge, deep quarry on the right which is attractively landscaped with a pool at the bottom. Soon the track zigzags steeply downhill

to reach a spot near the bottom of the quarry **D**. Do not take the last sharp turn to the right, which leads to the quarry, but keep ahead along a much narrower path – take care here as the ground slopes steeply away from the path in places – which winds and undulates through woodland along the side of the hill to reach a path junction.

Here bear slightly right, ignoring two descending paths on the immediate right, to continue along a steadily ascending path – with grand views all the while to the right over Great Malvern and the Vale of Severn – taking the right-hand path at a fork by a metal seat. This pleasant, grassy,

well-wooded path heads gently downhill, curving right, below the face of the hill, to join a track. Continue along the track, which winds through more attractive woodland, to St Ann's Well. In the nineteenth century buildings were erected over the well for the use of the increasing number of visitors coming to take the waters; nowadays they serve as a café.

At the well **E** turn right to follow the well-used broad tarmac track which winds downhill to a lane. Turn right at a footpath sign, heading down a drive towards a large house, and go down some steps to the left of the gateway to the house, turning left and continuing down a flight of steps to

St Ann's Well

reach the road directly in front of the Abbey Hotel and priory. Turn left for the short distance back to the start. ☐

For much of the way along the main ridge of the Malvern Hills, Great Malvern with its medieval priory can be seen and there are extensive views across the Vale of Severn

Birks of Aberfeldy

This is an extension of a popular 200-year-old walk through the steep, wooded gorge of the Moness Den with its sheer rockfaces and noisy waterfalls. It takes in wide, high-level views over Strath Tay and the town of Aberfeldy. The paths along the edges of rock precipices have been made easier and safer with handrails, and with walkways bridging awkward places. It is, however, still quite a steep walk, ascending some 600 feet (183 m) in 1 mile (1.5 km). The Birks of Aberfeldy are the subject of a Burns poem of the same name.

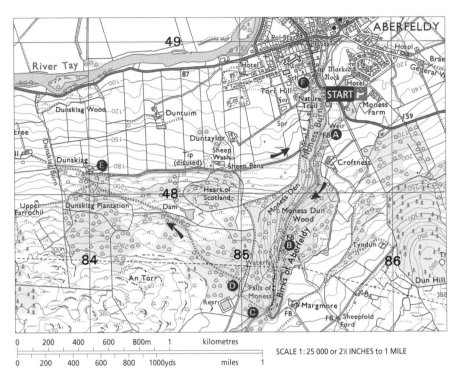

Start	Birks of Aberfeldy car park, Crieff road, Aberfeldy
Distance	4 miles (6.5 km)
Approximate time	2½ hours
Parking	Birks of Aberfeldy car park
Refreshments	Pubs and café in Aberfeldy
Ordnance Survey maps	Rangefinder 52 (Pitlochry & Aberfeldy), Pathfinder 323, NN 84/94 (Aberfeldy)

SCALE 1: 25 000 or 2½ INCHES to 1 MILE

The Moness Burn, packed with boulders

Soon after the waymarked footpath leaves the car park at the foot of the glen it splits into two. Take the left fork over a footbridge **Ⓐ** above a small waterfall. After a stand of beech trees the path starts climbing through the natural woodland of the glen, a mix of wych-elm, ash, willow, rowan, guelder rose, oak and hazel. Ferns of many varieties are prolific. Wintergreen and wood vetch prosper in the wet ground and flower from June to August. The Moness Burn is chock-a-block with huge boulders, many of which must weigh two or three tons. The glen was formed by the gouging action of the retreating glaciers about 10,000 years ago, and the numerous waterfalls are formed by streams tumbling down the side of the glen and by the main burn flowing over bands of hard rock. But however hard rock is it will, little by little, be eroded by the action of water, especially when it freezes in a fissure, expands and cracks the rock. Chunks fall off and clutter the floor of the valley.

The burns falling down the rockside have been bridged, making the going easier and drier, and they also provide pretty sights, especially where steps and bridges take the path higher in a spiral staircase configuration round the falling water. Nearing the top of the glen, the path follows a hairpin bend **Ⓑ** to climb suddenly much higher, but there is another path which keeps straight ahead for a few yards to a fenced rock platform overlooking a flight of five cascades, each falling into a pill. Take the hairpin bend. The path goes by steps and bridges to the top edge of the glen, where the trees give way to fields. Ahead now, well below the path, are the Falls of Moness, dropping 80 feet (24 m) over a stone sill. Continue along the path and then go up onto the opposite flank of the glen where there is a closer view from a bridge spanning the top of the falls.

From here there is a straightforward forest path leading downhill back to the car park, but ignore this route back. At the top of the short slope up from the bridge, turn off left onto a narrow footpath **Ⓒ**, little more than a rabbit-run, which takes you uphill through a broadleaved wood and onto the farm road from Urlar. Turn right along this road and go downhill for about 100 yards (91 m) and through a gate on the left **Ⓓ**. You are then on another farm road, mostly grass, which descends gently through thinly spaced trees for nearly 1 mile (1.5 km) to Dunskiag **Ⓔ**, a fairly large farmhouse with outbuildings, all empty and forlorn on the hillside overlooking the River Tay. The farm road from Farrochill to the west passes Dunskiag and takes you all the way back into Aberfeldy. It is a road with uninterrupted views to the north and provides plenty to look at. The tip of Ben Lawers can be glimpsed to the west and a little to its right is the top of Schiehallion. Immediately across the strath is Castle Menzies, a sixteenth-century fortified tower-house now in the care of the clan society and open to the public. Next to it is the tiny village of Weem, with the Weem, a whitewashed old inn, clearly visible. It was there that General Wade lodged while building his military roads and bridges hereabouts, and there is a portrait of him on the outside wall.

Approaching Aberfeldy on the latter part of the walk there are expansive and uninterrupted views up and down Strath Tay

Aberfeldy is seen in a curve of the Tay, which is crossed by Wade's bridge built in 1733 to a design by William Adam, father of Robert Adam, Scotland's most famous architect. It was the most ambitious of thirty-five major bridges along a network of 250 miles (402 km) of new roads and the only one surviving as a functioning highway. There is a strange obelisk at all four corners of the centre arch, and the stone parapet is so high that it cannot be looked over. Its strategic importance in Scotland's first proper road system is obvious to see from the high level of the farm road. To the right of Wade's bridge, on the edge of the golf-course, is a pedestrian suspension bridge – the first in the world to be constructed of glass fibre.

The farm road drops down into the outskirts of the town to become a street, ending at the junction with the Crieff road **F**, the A826, running south from the town centre. Turn right here and the car park is 200 yards (183 m) on the right. ☐

Broadway and Broadway Tower

This walk follows a simple 'across, up, across and down' pattern, with the easy downhill stretch at the end. Starting in the centre of Broadway at the foot of the Cotswold escarpment, the walk first heads across fields to Broadway Old Church, then climbs steeply through woodland to reach the top of the scarp. It continues along the edge to Broadway Tower, considered one of the finest viewpoints in England, before descending back into the village. On the latter part of the walk a magnificent view across the Vale of Evesham stretches out in front all the while.

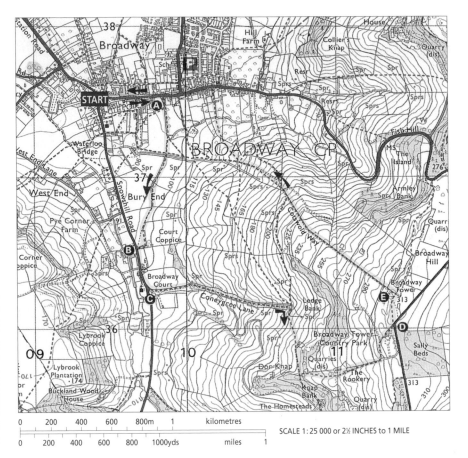

Start	Broadway
Distance	4 miles (6.5 km)
Approximate time	2 hours
Parking	Broadway
Refreshments	Pubs, cafés and restaurants at Broadway, café at Broadway Tower Country Park
Ordnance Survey maps	Landranger 150 (Worcester & The Malverns), Pathfinder 1043, SP 03/13 (Broadway & Chipping Campden)

SCALE 1:25 000 or 2½ INCHES to 1 MILE

Broadway nestles below the escarpment at the foot of steep Fish Hill on the edge of the Vale of Evesham. It is one of the showplace villages of the Cotswolds – as its teeming crowds and traffic readily testify – despite lacking the normal attractions of a river, an outstanding building or any well-known amenities. Its popularity lies in its situation and the

The Cotswold village of Broadway

overall charm of its buildings, mostly handsome seventeenth- and eighteenth-century houses. A wide, dignified, long high street, the Broad Way, slopes down and broadens out to a triangular green around which are grouped houses and cottages, inns and tearooms, and gift and antique shops. It was its position as a staging post on the main coach route between London and Worcester that brought prosperity to Broadway in the eighteenth century; later it became a fashionable place for writers and artists, starting with William Morris, one of the Pre-Raphaelite fraternity and a highly influential artist, craftsman and critic of Victorian industrialism.

The starting point is at the bottom of the long high street by the war memorial. Walk up the street and opposite the Horse and Hound Inn turn right at a signpost to 'Recreation Ground and Old Church' **Ⓐ**,

along a path between high walls on the left and a hedge on the right. This soon continues through an attractive avenue of trees and along the edge of a recreation ground, by a metal fence on the right. To the right the tower of the nineteenth-century New Church stands out prominently. Climb a stile, continue along clear grassy paths over a succession of stiles and across several fields, following yellow waymarks all the time. In the last field follow the field boundary round to the right to go through a gate and onto a road **Ⓑ**.

Turn left along the road for about 300 yards (274 m), passing the impressive buildings of Broadway Court on the right and beyond that the delightful, attractive Old Church dedicated to St Eadburgha, ¾ mile (1.25 km) south of the village. It is an imposing cruciform building with a fine fourteenth-century tower and the interior

is a fascinating and harmonious blend of Norman and Gothic features. Opposite the church turn left through ornamental gates **Ⓒ**, at a public footpath sign to Broadway Tower, along a wide tree-lined track, passing to the left of a lodge. Follow this pleasant track uphill for just over ½ mile (0.75 km) to a T-junction, and turn right. Go through a gate about 50 yards (46 m) ahead and bear left, still walking uphill, across a field towards a bungalow. Bear right in front of the bungalow, pass through a gate and keep ahead to a metal gate at the edge of woodland. Do not go through that gate but turn left through another one along another uphill track, later joining a lane and continuing to the top of the escarpment.

Just before reaching Broadway Country Park car park turn left over a stile **Ⓓ** to walk along the edge of the scarp. A ladder-stile on the right leads to a café; the walk

From Broadway Tower on the Cotswold escarpment there is a superb view over the Vale of Evesham. This is one of the finest viewpoints in England

keeps ahead through a gate and along a grassy path, by a fence on the right, to Broadway Tower which at a height of 1,024 feet (312 m) is the second highest point in the Cotswolds. The views from here over the Vale of Evesham, Broadway, Bredon Hill and the distant Malverns are magnificent, and in exceptionally clear conditions the Shropshire Hills and Black Mountains can also be seen. The tower is a folly, built in 1798 by James Wyatt for the Earl of Coventry, as a present for his wife, and is undoubtedly one of the most impressive viewpoints in England. Since 1972 it has been the focal point of a small country park and houses exhibitions about the tower itself, William Morris and the Cotswold woollen industry.

Now comes the easy descent to Broadway village along part of the Cotswold Way. Turn left past the tower **E** down to a stile in the corner of a field, climb it and continue downhill, across a succession of fields, through several gates and over stiles, following yellow-waymarked signs all the way and with outstanding views ahead over the Vale of Evesham and beyond. After crossing an area of rough pasture go through a gap in a hedge where the yellow waymarks show that the path divides. Here bear right, heading diagonally across the field to climb a stile in the bottom corner. Continue across a brook, over two more stiles and on to the road where you turn left down the high street to return to the starting point. □

Fan y Big and Taf Fechan Forest

After an initial steep climb, the rest of this walk in the heart of the Brecon Beacons is relatively relaxing. The climb is to the ridges of Craig y Fan Ddu and later Graig Fan Las which the walk follows to reach the main north-facing escarpment of the Beacons. After a dramatic stretch along the curving rim of the escarpment to the summit of Fan y Big, the route descends to the 'Gap Road' and follows this trackway, which is thought to be Roman, above the Neuadd reservoirs. Finally there is a pleasant, scenic stroll along the Taff Trail through the woodlands of Taf Fechan Forest. Although a comparatively easy mountain walk, much of it is along the edge of steep escarpments and therefore do not attempt it in winter or in misty weather unless properly experienced and equipped for such conditions.

Start	Torpantau
Distance	8 miles (12.75 km)
Approximate time	4½ hours
Parking	Forestry Commission's Talybont car park at Torpantau
Refreshments	None
Ordnance Survey maps	Landranger 160 (Brecon Beacons), Outdoor Leisure 11 (Brecon Beacons – Central area)

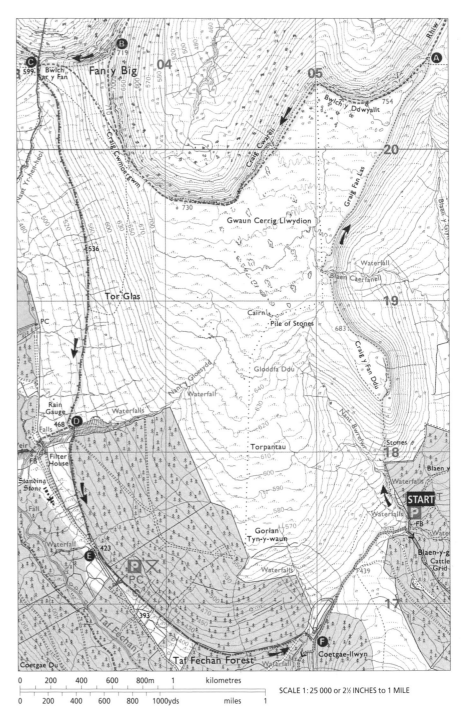

Begin by walking back to the car park entrance and immediately turn right onto an uphill path, by a wire fence on the right and above a steam and waterfalls on the left. Follow the wire fence as it curves round to the right and after it ends keep straight ahead, more steeply uphill, to

The view over the Upper Neuadd reservoir

reach a cairn at the top of the ridge. To the right there are superb views over the Talybont valley to the long ridges of the Black Mountains on the horizon.

Continue along the peaty, badly drained ridge top of Craig y Fan Ddu and ahead is the impressive, sweeping, smooth curve of the ridge of Graig Fan Las. Later bear right to ford a stream and continue, curving gradually right along Graig Fan Las and enjoying the magnificent open, empty views to the right over mountain and forest. When you eventually reach the main escarpment of the Brecon Beacons turn sharp left **A**.

Keep along the clear, well-used path to the summit of Fan y Big, following the edge of the escarpment as it bends left and later curves right around the head of the valley of Cwm Oergwm. This is a typical Beacons landscape of sweeping, bare, smooth curves, steep escarpments, flat summits and wide vistas, with views beyond of the gentler scenery of the Usk valley and the houses of Brecon. On reaching Fan y Big's rather unremarkable summit **B** turn sharp left, still walking along the edge of the escarpment, to descend into the broad col of Bwlch ar y Fan which lies between Fan y Big and Cribyn. Ahead looms the abrupt and

A typical landscape in the heart of the Brecon Beacons – looking along the escarpment from Fan y Big to Cribyn and beyond to Pen y Fan, highest point in southern Britain

daunting-looking peak of Cribyn, to the left the Upper Neuadd reservoir can be seen and to the right there is a view down Cwm Cynwyn to the Usk valley.

At the col turn left along a broad, flat, stony track **C**, which is thought to be of Roman origin and is usually referred to as the Gap Road because it makes use of the gap in the escarpment. Follow this

trackway above the Upper Neuadd reservoir and after 1½ miles (2.5 km), where the main track turns right, there is a choice of routes **D**. If the stream below is fordable, bear left and head steeply down a rocky track to ford it, head up the other side and continue along the right-hand edge of conifers to descend gently to a road. Otherwise, follow the main track

to the right down to a metal gate, turn left onto a path in front of it, cross the stream, climb a stile and continue along the road ahead. The track and road meet at a Taff Trail footpath sign **E**.

Here keep straight ahead along a flat, grassy track which is part of the Taff Trail. It runs to the left of the road, by a wire fence on the right and along the edge

of the conifers of Taf Fechan Forest. Ahead are most attractive views towards the Talybont reservoir. The track passes through several gates and continues through woodland, eventually bending right to cross a stream and rejoin the road **F**. Turn left and follow the road uphill for just over ½ mile (0.75 km) to return to the start.

Heritage walks

The landscape is both an ancient and an ever-changing phenomenon and one of the many delights of walking in Britain is a constant awareness of the past. Even a quick look at an Ordnance Survey map reveals the long history of people's contribution to the landscape, ranging from prehistoric chalk figures and Roman defences to Victorian railway viaducts, and from medieval castles and abbeys to twentieth-century motorway bridges. Even the footpaths that we tread are part of our national heritage, some following the line of ancient long-distance trails, others being old drove roads by which cattle were driven on the hoof, and most are simply the routes by which local people travelled to work or their nearest market town.

The chance to explore places of historic interest adds an extra dimension to a walk, and seeing historic sites from a distance reveals their place in the landscape. Some parts of the country in which famous artists and writers lived have come to be indelibly associated with them and walking through them, as in one of the following walks, in 'Constable Country', allows appreciation of the landscape that inspired them.

Many historic and architectural treasures have particularly attractive settings and over time have become an integral part of the landscape. The walk that starts by Ribblehead Viaduct illustrates this. At first many people regarded such structures as ugly intrusions, but now they are cherished as being handsome in themselves and an important part of our national heritage.

FLORA AND FAUNA

Heritage walks often traverse ancient tracks, passing through many types of country. In the uplands well-worn trails lead over springy, close-cropped turf with starry tormentil flowers sparkling in the grass and wheatears flitting from one out-cropping rock to another.

On the other hand, many lowland pathways lead through lush pastures and frequently accompany slow-flowing rivers where herons *(above)* fish in quiet backwaters and where in summer the banks are hidden beneath a wealth of flowers such as hemp agrimony and purple loosestrife.

Hadrian's Wall
from Steel Rigg ●

● Ribblehead and
Chapel le Dale

Constable
Country
●

Carreg Cennen Castle ●

● Tintern Abbey and
the Devil's Pulpit

● Cerne Abbas and
Minterne Magna

Cerne Abbas and Minterne Magna

Historic interest and superb scenery are combined on this splendid downland walk. From Cerne Abbas a footpath heads up onto the downs, passing below the prehistoric figure of the Cerne Giant, and continues across open country and through woodland, with fine sweeping views, before descending into Minterne Magna. A short, easy climb onto a ridge is followed by a descent into the tiny hamlet of Up Cerne and a final stretch along a quiet lane back to Cerne Abbas. It is on this last leg that you see the classic view of the Cerne Giant on the opposite hillside.

Start	Kettle Bridge picnic area on the edge of Cerne Abbas
Distance	6½ miles (10.5 km)
Approximate time	3½ hours
Parking	Kettle Bridge picnic area
Refreshments	Pubs and cafés at Cerne Abbas
Ordnance Survey maps	Landranger 194 (Dorchester & Weymouth), Pathfinder 1299, ST 60/70 (Cerne Abbas & Hazelbury Bryan)

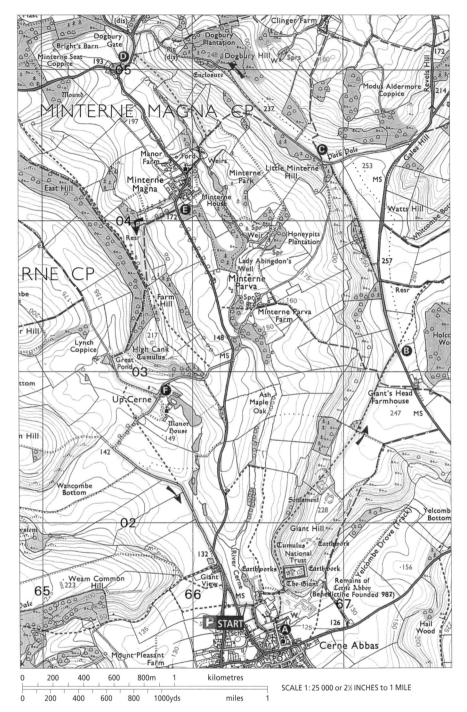

From the Kettle Bridge picnic area turn left along the lane for a few yards and just before a bridge turn right to follow a delightful tarmac path beside the tree-lined River Cerne into the village. Where the path forks turn left over a footbridge and continue along the path ahead to emerge in Abbey Street **Ⓐ**. The church and village centre are to the right.

It is difficult to believe that the now quiet backwater of Cerne Abbas was once an important centre for the leather and

Attractive houses at Cerne Abbas

brewing industries. It declined in the nineteenth century and today is an exceptionally attractive village of stone and flint with some fine Georgian houses and, unusual for Dorset, a group of timber-fronted cottages in Abbey Street. The mainly fifteenth-century church is a graceful, spacious building with an imposing west tower. Of the once great Benedictine monastery, founded in 987, there are only fragmentary remains of the abbey itself, but a gatehouse and guest-house survive, and an impressive fourteenth-century tithe barn on the other side of the village.

Turn left towards the abbey ruins and just after passing to the left of a duckpond turn right through a metal gate in an archway; follow a diagonal path across a cemetery to go through a similar metal gate in another archway. Keep in the same direction across a field, with the abbey remains on the left, and head uphill

towards trees and the base of the hill on which the Cerne Giant is carved. Climb a stile and, ignoring another stile on the left, continue quite steeply uphill along a clearly defined path to a Cerne Giant National Trust sign.

Continue along a path by the wire fence enclosing the giant on the right. The possibility of damage by visitors' feet means that it cannot be inspected closely and it is impossible to see anything as you pass below. All the way along there are grand views to the left over the wide and sweeping Cerne valley. Where the wire fence ends keep ahead, contouring along the side of Giant Hill, roughly parallel to a hedge below on the left. Bear slightly away from the hedge to follow a broad green ledge over the shoulder of the hill, continuing up between bushes into an open grassy area. Now keep along the right-hand edge of gorse bushes to climb a stile, turn half-left and head across a large open field – there may be no visible path – making for a waymarked gatepost by the right-hand edge of a group of trees and in front of an open-sided barn. Continue in the direction of the yellow (not the blue) waymarking arrows along the left hand edge of a field, by a hedge on the left, now following an obvious path to a stile, and climb it onto a road **B**.

Turn left along the road for ¼ mile (0.5 km) and at the end of a group of fine old trees on the left turn left through a gate, then turn half-right and head across to a fence corner. Go through a gate and continue along the left-hand edge of a field high above the valley, by a wire fence on the left, later keeping above a narrow belt of woodland on the left to reach a T-junction **C**. Here turn left to walk along a fine, broad, ridge-top track, with splendid views on both sides over rolling country; to the left Minterne House is prominent in the valley below. Follow the track through a circular wooded area, which contains the earthworks of Dogbury Camp, after which it heads downhill to a road.

Turn left onto the road and at the left-hand side of a house turn left again through a wooden gate **D**. Go through a waymarked metal gate a few yards in front and head straight across a large sloping field – there is no path – keeping roughly parallel to and about 100 yards (91 m) above a fence on the right. Go through the next metal gate and keep in the same direction across the next field, parallel to a wire fence on the right, along a narrow but discernible path that bears slightly left to pass through another metal gate.

Near the end of the walk comes this striking view of the Cerne Giant, a prehistoric fertility symbol cut out of the chalk hillside

Afterwards the path bears right and continues across the next field to a metal gate; go through it and turn right along a downhill track. Ahead is Minterne House, a large mansion built around the beginning of the century. It is not open to the public but the gardens can be visited during the summer. The track bears left to cross a footbridge over a stream and continues into the village of Minterne Magna, passing the small fifteenth-century church.

Turn left along the main road that curves to the right through the village, and just after it bends to the left turn right through a metal gate **E** and walk along a straight, tree-lined track, heading up to another metal gate. Go through that, turn left for a few yards by a fence on the left, and then bear right to head diagonally uphill across

a sloping field, making for a metal gate in the far corner. Go through and keep in the same direction across the corner of the next field to go through a waymarked gate onto a track a few yards ahead. Turn left and almost immediately bear right at a fork along a grassy, tree-lined track that heads downhill, curving right to a T-junction in front of the Great Pond.

Turn left along a tarmac track into the secluded thatched hamlet of Up Cerne **F**. Here there is the traditional and highly picturesque scene of manor house and church side by side, beautifully situated above a lake. The church dates from the fifteenth century and the manor house mainly from the sixteenth century, but both were heavily restored in the nineteenth century.

Turn right along a quiet, narrow lane, at first uphill then gently downhill and finally around a sharp left-hand bend to continue to the main road. Bear right and about 100 yards (91 m) ahead is the junction and layby at Giant View. From here is the best view of the Cerne Giant, a prehistoric male nude figure 180 feet (55 m) tall, cut out of the chalk hillside. The erect phallus indicates that the figure was associated with fertility, and not surprisingly many stories have grown up around it, notably that making love on the figure or simply sitting on the tip of the phallus was a cure for barrenness.

From Giant View take the left fork, signposted to the village centre, and then the first turning on the left to return to the starting point. □

Hadrian's Wall from Steel Rigg

This walk provides the opportunity of seeing the most dramatic stretch of Hadrian's Wall. Choose your time to undertake the route carefully – it is wise to avoid bank holiday afternoons! Early mornings or evenings are ideal, the low light dramatising the landscape and highlighting beautiful Crag Lough. Also avoid very windy days. The return leg on the north side of Hadrian's Wall is pleasant walking, with wonderful views of the wall and the whinstone ridge on which it was built.

Hadrian's Wall stretches 73½ miles (118 km) from coast to coast

Start	Steel Rigg, 1 mile (1·5 km) north of national park information centre at Once Brewed, Military Road, Bardon Mill
Distance	5 miles (8 km)
Approximate time	2½ hours
Parking	National park car park at Steel Rigg
Refreshments	None
Ordnance Survey maps	Landrangers 86 (Haltwhistle, Bewcastle & Alston) and 87 (Hexham & Haltwhistle), Pathfinder 546, NY 66/76 (Haltwhistle & Gilsland)

Pass through the kissing-gate in the lower right corner of the car park and follow the path to the wall at Peel Gap. Steps help the steep ascent to Peel Crags, the start of a series of switchback climbs and descents along perhaps the most photographed section of Hadrian's Wall. The spectacular view is of great interest geologically and strategically: the scarp of the Great Whin Sill is seen rising precipitously above Crag Lough while the dip slope falls gently away to the south. Look back too at the climb you have just made. It started from a vulnerable point in the wall, a gap where the Romans protected the wall by digging a deep ditch on its northern side. This can still be clearly seen.

The path soon descends again, to a gap known as Cat Stairs where there is a tumble of stones which have fallen from the wall through the ages. The abundance of wild flowers on this rocky habitat is attributed to the mortar which was used

in the construction of the wall, its lime modifying the composition of the soil. Another climb follows and then a further steep descent, this time to Castle Nick.

The gap here was protected by Milecastle 39 which has been recently excavated. Although there are minor deviations in size and design, all of the milecastles along the wall had basic features in common. Built to accommodate eight soldiers, they were gatehouses allowing access from one side of the wall to the other. Thus the most important feature was the gatetower itself where the gates opened outwards on the north side of the wall. There were also living quarters, a storehouse, an oven and, in the north-east corner, steps leading to the battlemented parapet of the wall itself which was generally at least 19½ feet (6 m) high. All this was surrounded on the south side by an enclosing bailey wall, also with parapet walk and crenellations and

a gate on its south side. As the name implies, milecastles were situated 1 mile (1·5 km) apart.

The path climbs again and then drops down steps to a circular stone wall which protects a sycamore tree. Pass to the north side of the wall, following the waymarks. You are soon on the crags high above the lough. Heather-topped Barcombe Hill to the south is where the stone used in the wall was quarried. The communications tower to the north-west stands on the hill memorably named Hopealone.

The path descends through National Trust woodland (planted, not a natural feature) and skirts the boundary of Hotbank Farm before a taxing climb alongside the wall up to Hotbank Crags. The view from the top is a classic – one often used to illustrate Hadrian's Wall on postcards and brochures. To the west the wall snakes its way towards the horizon above the sparkling waters of Crag Lough – on a clear day the Lakeland summits of Blencathra and Skiddaw can be seen. To the north are the twin Greenlee and

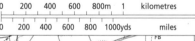

SCALE 1:31 250 or about 2 INCHES to 1 MILE

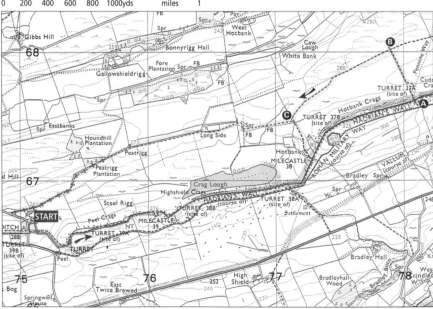

Broomlee loughs, and Housesteads car park can be seen ahead, heralding the most popular part of Hadrian's Wall.

For a short distance the wall is unreconstructed, and the path alongside dips down sharply to Ranishaw Gap which is where the Pennine Way joins with the wall to follow it westwards. There is a gate **A**, and steps on the left. Cross the wall by these but do not follow the waymark which points out the course of the Pennine Way towards Broomlee Lough north-eastwards. Instead follow the line of a broken-down wall, keeping it to the left, so that you are walking directly away from Hadrian's Wall at this point. At what looks like a very ornate cattle-shelter **B**, but was in fact a lime-kiln, turn left to follow a mini-escarpment westwards.

On the left is a planting of conifers, and Greenlee Lough is on the right. Hadrian's Wall from here looks a forbidding defence-work which must have deterred many a raiding party. The walking is easy on springy turf. Another path joins from the right as ours bends to the left, and turns again to reach a stone wall and a farm gate **C**. Turn to the right following a waymark pointing across a large pasture (a notice requests people to walk in single file to avoid damaging the hay crop). From here the cliffs rearing above Crag Lough are truly impressive.

Cross the next meadow following a well-used but still grassy path towards the crags on top of Steel Rigg. The path bends to the right to cross slightly boggy ground to reach a gate. Use the adjacent ladder-stile and follow the right of way which now heads towards a cattle byre, keeping close to the wall on the right. Almost imperceptibly the path becomes a track. Pass Peatrigg Plantation and continue along the track until it reaches the road below Steel Rigg car park and turn left to return to the start. ☐

RIGHT *The most spectacular part of Hadrian's Wall, seen from Peel Crags*

Tintern Abbey and the Devil's Pulpit

Every ingredient that goes to create a varied, satisfying and memorable walk is present here: a peaceful riverside path below steep wooded cliffs, a climb through attractive woodland to a magnificent vantage point, a descent across more open country and a final relaxing stroll across meadows bordering the River Wye. As a bonus there is of course Tintern Abbey itself, one of the most beautiful and superbly situated monastic remains in the country.

Start	Tintern
Distance	7 miles (11.25 km)
Approximate time	3½ hours
Parking	Parking spaces beside road at Tintern
Refreshments	Pubs and cafés at Tintern, pub at Brockweir, café at Tintern Station
Ordnance Survey maps	Landranger 162 (Gloucester & Forest of Dean), Outdoor Leisure 14 (Wye Valley & Forest of Dean)

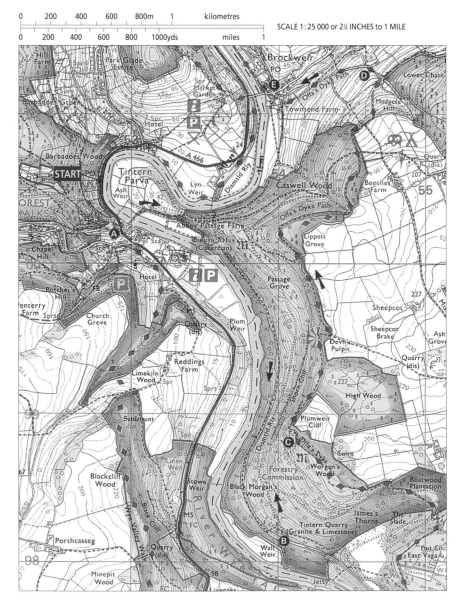

Begin by walking southwards along the main road and soon Tintern Abbey comes into sight. Its setting on the Welsh side of the river, with the steep, thickly wooded cliffs on the opposite English bank making a dramatic backcloth, is superb. Tintern was a Cistercian monastery, founded by Walter de Clare, Lord of Chepstow, in 1131, and had an apparently uneventful history until its dissolution by Henry VIII in 1536. The remains are most impressive, especially the majestic church, rebuilt in the late thirteenth century, which is almost intact save for roofs and windows. Its walls still rise to their full height and much of the delicate window tracery survives.

Continue along the road if you wish to visit the abbey. Otherwise take the first turning on the left **Ⓐ**, passing Abbey Mill on the right, and cross the footbridge over the River Wye. Continue along the wooded track ahead, which curves to the right to run roughly parallel to the river, and keep along this track, once part of the picturesque Wye Valley Railway, for nearly 2 miles (3.25 km), at the base of wooded cliffs on the left and with the river on the right. Gaps in the trees in the initial stages provide a few glimpses of the river and abbey ruins.

Take the left-hand track at a fork, following the direction of yellow arrows, and climb gently to the next yellow waymark. Here turn sharp left along an uphill track **Ⓑ**, following a permissive route and looking out for yellow waymarks all the time, to reach a T-junction of tracks. Cross over and take the narrow path ahead that leads steeply uphill through dense but attractive woodland to another T-junction. Turn left and head slightly downhill to a waymark and here turn right along a narrow, winding, uphill, stepped path. At the next waymark you join Offa's Dyke Path **Ⓒ**; keep ahead and follow it as it twists and turns through the trees high above the valley to arrive at the vantage point of the Devil's Pulpit. From here there is a glorious view over the Wye Valley to the wooded slopes beyond, with the abbey ruins immediately below. According to legend the devil tried to entice the monks from their duties at this spot, hence its name.

Continue above the valley and through more lovely woodland, following Offa's Dyke Path waymarks all the while and soon starting to descend. At a signpost ignore the left-hand turn to Tintern and keep ahead along Offa's Dyke Path, following the signs to Brockweir and St Briavels, later going down steps to a wooden barrier. Go through and keep

The River Wye at Brockweir

straight ahead at a junction of paths, now heading gently downhill along the right-hand edge of woodland and bearing right to a stile. Climb it, continue along the top edge of the valley and at an Offa's Dyke Path waymark bear left away from the wire fence on the right along a rocky path which heads downhill.

Continue in a straight line across a field, in the direction indicated by yellow-topped posts, and at the bottom corner climb the stile and turn left onto a broad track. Head down to a signpost where Offa's Dyke Path divides and bear left **D** in the direction of the sign 'Offa's Dyke Path via River Wye'. Go through a gate, on through another one and continue, passing stable buildings on the right, to go through yet another gate and down to another signpost. Ignoring the left hand turn to Tintern on the signpost, turn right between farm buildings and continue along a tarmac drive to the road at Brockweir **E**.

Turn left along the road, cross the river and turn left over a stile, at a public footpath sign to Tintern, to descend steps. At the bottom there is a choice of routes. One route is to turn left, climb a stile and then turn right to follow a pleasant path across riverside meadows. The alternative is to keep along the track straight ahead, which passes through the disused Tintern Station, to rejoin the riverside path by the supports of a former railway bridge. The old Victorian station at Tintern has been attractively restored as a visitor and information centre and picnic site.

Where the two alternative routes reunite, climb a stile and keep along the riverbank, curving right to cross a footbridge over a ditch and continuing up to another stile. Climb over, walk through the churchyard of Tintern's small parish church and follow yellow arrows between houses to the main road. Keep ahead to return to the parking area. □

RIGHT *The superb view over Tintern Abbey and the Wye Valley from the Devil's Pulpit*

Carreg Cennen Castle

The major attraction of this popular and well-waymarked walk in the western foothills of the Black Mountain is the ever-changing views of Carreg Cennen Castle, perched on its precipitous rock, from many different angles. The finale is superb – a steady ascent through beautiful sloping woodland to reach the castle entrance.

Start	Carreg Cennen Castle
Distance	4 miles (6.5 km)
Approximate time	2 hours
Parking	Car park at Carreg Cennen Castle
Refreshments	Farm café next to car park
Ordnance Survey maps	Landranger 159 (Swansea, Gower & surrounding area), Outdoor Leisure 12 (Brecon Beacons – Western area)

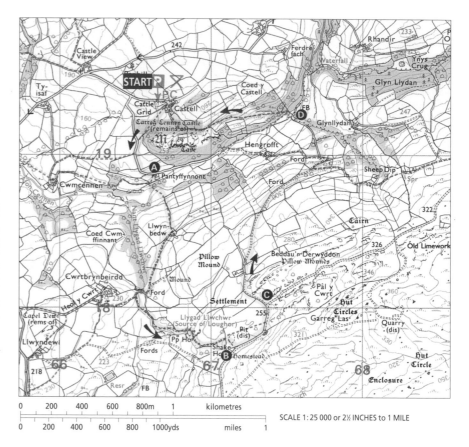

SCALE 1: 25 000 or 2½ INCHES to 1 MILE

One of the most dramatically sited castles in Britain, Carreg Cennen occupies a 300-foot- (91 m) high exposed vertical limestone outcrop above the Cennen valley. It is everyone's idea of what a ruined castle should be like; it is even complete with an underground passage, hewn from the rock, which leads down into a cave. Originally a Welsh fortress, stronghold of the Lords Rhys, it was taken by the English and rebuilt and strengthened in the late thirteenth and early fourteenth centuries. Most of its extensive remains belong to that period. Despite its apparent impregnability, it was besieged and captured on a number of occasions and passed through several hands until being largely demolished to prevent its use by brigands after the Wars of the Roses.

At the far end of the car park go through a gate into the farmyard of Castle Farm. Do not continue ahead between the farm buildings towards the castle, but turn right

Carreg Cennen Castle is the archetypal ruined castle, complete with underground passage

and go through another gate adjacent to a barn. Head downhill across a field, making for a stile and footpath sign in the bottom left-hand corner – like most of the signs on this walk it has a castle symbol on it. Climb the stile and turn left along a narrow lane.

Ignore the first stile on the right and follow the lane downhill, curving left to reach a second stile just before a cottage, at a public footpath sign to Llwyn-bedw Ⓐ. Turn right over the stile, head downhill across a field, bearing slightly right to climb a stile in the field corner, and continue along a steep downhill path to climb another stile at the bottom. Continue across the next field, cross a footbridge over the River Cennen and bear slightly left to head uphill to a stile. Climb it and continue steeply uphill, keeping parallel with a wire fence and line of trees on the left, towards a farm. In front of the buildings turn right to walk along a track, initially across sloping fields and later

through an attractive area of scattered trees. After fording a stream the track bends to the right and then curves left to reach a footpath sign a few yards ahead.

Turn left here over a stile and walk along a track, by a hedge-bank on the right, bearing slightly left to cross a footbridge over a narrow stream and continuing to a stile. Climb it and bear slightly right along an enclosed track; this later emerges briefly into a more open area before continuing as a tree-lined route by the infant River Loughor on the right, a most attractive part of the walk. Climb a stile and if you want to see the source of the Loughor which issues from a cave here, another stile immediately to the right gives access to it.

Continue along the track, which curves slightly left and winds gently uphill, by a wire fence on the right. It then turns left to continue initially by a hedge-bank on the right, and later it veers left away from it to a stile. Climb the stile, bear right to pass between two hollows and head across to climb a stile onto a lane **B**.

Turn left, climb a stile beside a cattle-grid and continue along the lane as far as a right-hand bend **C**. Here keep ahead along a track, by a wire fence and hedge-bank on the right. To the right are the Pillow Mounds, long grassy mounds that look like burial chambers but which were artificial rabbit warrens made by local people in the nineteenth century to ensure a regular supply of fresh meat. The track curves left to a stile; climb it, keep ahead to climb another and continue straight across the middle of a field, bearing slightly left to a gate.

Go through, continue along the left-hand edge of a field, by a wire fence on the left, climb a stile in the field corner by gorse bushes and keep ahead along a sunken grassy track above the steep Cennen valley, now heading downhill. At a fork take the left-hand, lower track which bends sharply left at a footpath sign and continues down to a crossroads of tracks and paths. Climb the stile straight ahead, descend steps and continue downhill along the stony, tree- and hedge-lined path, climbing another stile and keeping by a stream on the right. Turn right to cross a footbridge over the stream, turn left along the other bank, climb a stile and keep ahead to cross another footbridge over the River Cennen **D**.

Turn right and almost immediately turn sharp left, at a footpath sign to Carreg Cennen, onto an attractive path which heads steadily uphill through the lovely, sloping Coed y Castell (Castle Wood) towards the castle, a grand finale to the walk. Continue past the castle entrance at the top and follow the path as it descends, turning right through a kissing-gate, on through another one and down through Castle Farm to return to the start. □

RIGHT *The castle can be seen from almost all points on the walk*

Constable Country

This walk provides a leisurely way to appreciate the countryside that John Constable loved. Much of it is through beautiful meadows lined with willows, ashes and oaks whose ancestors may well have featured in some of the painter's work. There is the opportunity to explore East Bergholt or lovely Dedham before taking the path back to Flatford Mill along the banks of the Stour.

There is a fine mix of Tudor and Georgian buildings in Dedham

Start	Flatford Mill, near East Bergholt
Distance	5 miles (8 km)
Approximate time	2½ hours
Parking	Flatford Mill car park
Refreshments	Pubs and tearooms at East Bergholt and Dedham
Ordnance Survey maps	Landrangers 168 (Colchester & The Blackwater) and 169 (Ipswich & The Naze), Pathfinder 1053, TM 03/13 (Manningtree & Dedham)

From the car park take the clearly marked footpath to Flatford Mill. Do not cross the bridge at the bottom but bear left along the lane to Willy Lott's House. Turn left here onto the start of the Gibbonsgate Field Circular Walk, and at the end of the field turn right, in the direction signposted.

Take the footpath on the left **Ⓐ** before the electricity pylon, and then walk past the pylon, keeping the hedge to the right. Cross a new stile and turn left to follow the hedge past another stile and an inviting green lane on the left – Hog's Lane – which leads towards a wood. Do not take this but keep following the fine hedge on the left: this is an ideal field path with wide views to the estuary of the Stour. Cross a double

stile and continue to follow the hedge until you see cattle fencing and a gateway on the left **Ⓑ**. If the gate is closed cross the stile and plank bridge onto Dazeley's Lane, which goes to East Bergholt. A little way up the green lane there is an opening on the right which is an excellent viewpoint.

At the road turn left, and then after 50 yards (46 m) turn left again onto a very narrow path with gardens on each side **Ⓒ**. If you wish to explore East Bergholt, you can instead continue along the road to the

village and then take the Flatford Road to rejoin the route at **Ⓓ**.

The short path between the gardens continues across a field to a signpost to the right of the trees opposite. Go through this copse and along the narrow path beyond, heading towards houses. Cross Hog's Lane and follow the edge of two fields to reach Clapper Farm. Descend the drive 25 yards (23 m) to a ladder-stile and climb this and cross the paddock to another stile. Turn left to reach Flatford Road **Ⓓ** and go straight across onto another narrow field-edge path. This leads to a planting of young trees which discreetly veils a sewage works. Two more new stiles take the path across a loke and into a field. Cross this to yet another new stile which gives onto a lane. This is crossed directly to a gate of black-painted metal with stile attached. From here there is a classic view of Dedham Vale. Dedham church is to the left and Stratford St Mary church to the right.

Cross the lovely meadow to a bridge at the bottom **Ⓔ** and follow the track for 100 yards (91 m) until it divides by a clump of willows. Fork right, away from Fen Bridge, onto a path beneath the arched branches of the hedging trees. At the end of this path a stile gives access to a broad river meadow. The path soon reaches the riverbank and follows it to Dedham Bridge.

Cross the bridge. If you wish to visit the village with its beautiful church – Dedham

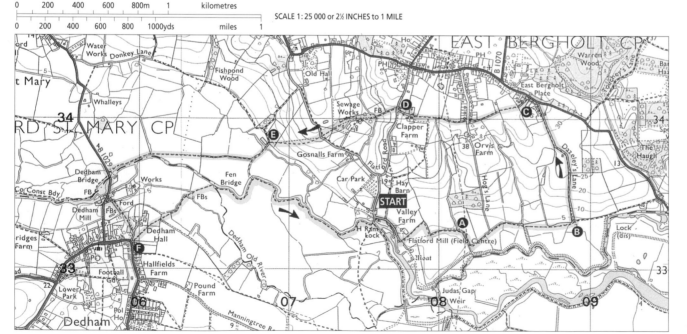

Willy Lott's House, seen here across the millpond at Flatford, featured in Constable's paintings – as did Flatford Mill itself. House and mill are now part of a field centre

is connected with another famous East Anglian artist, Sir Alfred Munnings – follow the road. If you would rather continue along footpaths, turn left off the road opposite the mill – which is now luxury flats – to cross the river by a footbridge. Immediately after the crossing take the footpath on the right. This skirts a field and then the garden and duckpond of Dedham Hall to reach Muniment House **F**, where those who explored Dedham would rejoin the route.

The return leg of the walk begins to the left of Muniment House where a gate opens onto a field track which passes behind Dedham Hall. Bear right away from the farmyard to reach a stile and a pathway leading down towards the river. This crosses a footbridge over the course of the old river and heads towards the riverbank which it reaches by a fine willow tree. Turn right to follow the winding course of the Stour to Flatford Mill, crossing the bridge there to return to the car park.

Ribblehead and Chapel le Dale

The Settle–Carlisle railway is the thread running through this undemanding though spectacular walk in the dramatic countryside of the 'Three Peaks' of Whernside, Ingleborough and Pen-y-ghent. In addition to these three natural phenomena the route is dominated for most of the way by the almost equally dramatic man-made structure of Ribblehead Viaduct. As well as being a major triumph of Victorian railway engineering, the viaduct blends in with its wild and bare surroundings so perfectly that it seems almost to be part of the landscape and even, it could be argued, to enhance it.

Start	Ribblehead
Distance	7 miles (11.25 km)
Approximate time	3½ hours
Parking	Opposite Station Inn at Ribblehead
Refreshments	Pub at Ribblehead, pub near Chapel le Dale
Ordnance Survey maps	Landranger 98 (Wensleydale & Upper Wharfedale), Outdoor Leisure 2 (Yorkshire Dales – Western area)

Take the broad track beside the Station Inn which heads across rough grassland towards the viaduct. Immediately there is a striking view of it, backed by the slopes of Whernside. The sight of a steam train chugging across it is even more dramatic and is guaranteed to attract an army of rail enthusiasts lying in wait with cameras poised.

Ribblehead Viaduct is the most impressive structure on the Settle–Carlisle line, which was built between 1869 and 1875 as part of a new route from London to Scotland, the last main line to be constructed during the Victorian railway era. Here, between the heads of the Ribble, Ure and Eden valleys, it crosses some of the wildest and most inhospitable Pennine moorland, and the physical and organisational problems of construction, and the human cost, were immense.

Follow the track under the massive arches of the viaduct **A**, which is ¼ mile (0.5 km) long and has a maximum height of 106 ft (32 m). Keep ahead through two gates and on past farm buildings to a footbridge over Waterscales Beck. Cross the bridge **B**, turn left through a gate along a tarmac farm road and pass through several more gates, eventually bearing left to join another farm road. Cross the beck again and continue ahead to a gate by the side of a cattle-grid. There is a superb view of Ingleborough directly ahead.

Bear right, away from the road, across the grass to a gate. Go through, keep ahead by a wall on the left, and at the corner of the wall continue across the usually dry bed of the stream in front to a ladder-stile. By now the landscape has gradually but noticeably changed from the bleak, bare, open moorland around Ribblehead to neat green fields criss-crossed by stone walls, with a few trees dotted around. Climb the ladder-stile and keep ahead, veering slightly to the left to a gate. Go through, continuing along a narrow, rocky path to a farm road, and turn left along it to the Ingleton–Hawes road **C**

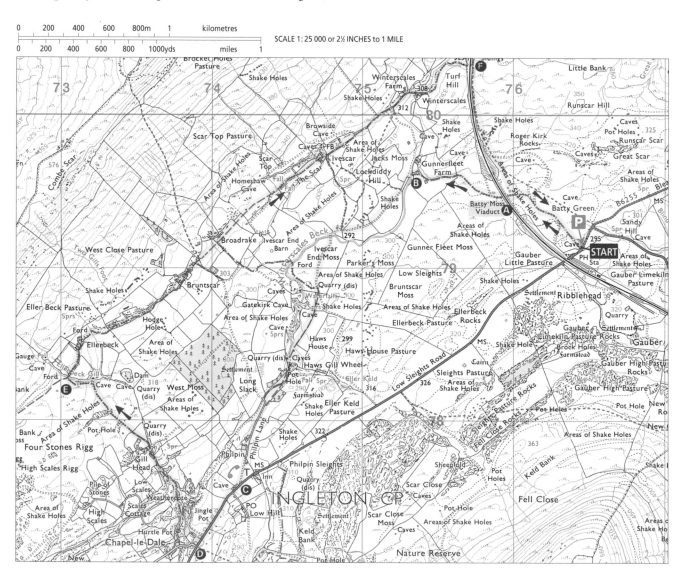

At the road turn right – the pub is a few yards to the left – down into the hamlet of Chapel le Dale; turn right along a lane **D** and over a stream to the church. It was to this tiny building that the bodies of navvies killed during the construction of the railway, and those of women and children who died in the appalling conditions of the shanty towns, were brought for burial. It has been estimated that over 200 bodies lie in unmarked graves in the churchyard, and inside the church is a memorial to all who lost their lives in the building of the Settle–Carlisle railway.

Turn right up the narrow lane in front of the church, continue through a gate, passing Hurtle Pot on the right, and where the lane ends keep ahead along a broad track signposted to Ellerbeck, through an attractive, rocky, tree-lined gorge. Passing a rather strange, futuristic bronze statue of a man – placed here after having been retrieved from Hurtle Pot – continue up into open country.

Bear right across a beck **E**, at a public footpath sign to Deepdale, and follow the track past farm buildings, veering right to a gate. Go through and keep along the clear, wide track, past several farms and through a series of gates, following the lower slopes of Whernside. From the track there are superb views over the dale towards the viaduct. After 1½ miles (2.5 km), at the point where the track bends sharply to the left, keep ahead a few yards to a gate at a public bridleway sign to Winterscales. Go through and continue ahead past more farms and through another succession of gates, keeping in a roughly straight line. Soon there is a fine view on the right of the third of the 'Three Peaks' – Peny-ghent –

unseen until now. At the second footbridge, by a group of farm buildings, keep ahead along a tarmac track which eventually reaches a hump-backed bridge over a stream. Cross it and bear left, following the stream, towards Blea Moor signal-box.

Bear right under the railway bridge and turn right to pick up a track running parallel to the railway **F**. For the final stretch of the walk keep by the railway, heading across rough grassland to meet the broad, well-surfaced track which leads back to the Station Inn and car park. ☐

A triumph of nineteenth-century railway engineering, Ribblehead Viaduct carries the Settle–Carlisle line across some of the wildest Pennine moorland

Walks on the wild side

Sooner or later some walkers who have served their apprenticeship on easier walks, then graduated to moorland and mountain slopes will get the urge to tackle some of the bleakest moorlands and highest peaks, the wild places of Britain. This final selection of walks is only for those who have gained a reasonable degree of physical fitness, have good map-reading skills and can navigate by using a compass. Otherwise, these walks should on no account be attempted, especially in bad weather such as strong winds and thick mist, and in wintry conditions.

For those who meet these requirements, though, the feeling of satisfaction and sense of achievement after accomplishing any of these walks is tremendous. Ben Nevis offers probably the greatest satisfaction of all, the conquest of Britain's highest peak. The climb to the summit of Helvellyn in the Lake District takes you along the exciting knife-edge ridge of Striding Edge, and the ascent of the twin Glyder peaks in Snowdonia involves a steep scramble up Bristly Ridge and an equally steep descent down the side of the dark, rocky cleft of the Devil's Kitchen. But high mountains are not the only examples of wild country and the

walk in the Cheviots explores of some of the loneliest moorland in Britain.

The thrill of meeting these challenges – finding your way across remote and rugged country, climbing and scrambling over rocks to lofty summits – and in the process viewing breathtaking scenery, is the greatest and most memorable of walking experiences.

FLORA AND FAUNA

Bleak, wind-swept mountaintops are inhospitable places, often bare apart from a mossy covering between the lichen-encrusted rocks. Nevertheless, where there are damp, north-facing cliffs, sheltered cracks accommodate plants such as the moss campion, and uninviting screes are frequently dotted with tufts of parsley fern.

Wildlife is sparse. Sometimes foxes *(above)* have earths on rock-strewn slopes, and aloft a passing raven may emit a guttural 'pruk-pruk', while soaring buzzards, hanging in the air, mew plaintively.

● Ben Nevis

● Hartside, Salters Road
and High Cantle

● Helvellyn

● The Glyders

The Glyders

The Glyders lie between the Llanberis and Nant Ffrancon passes and overlook the Snowdon range to the west and the Carneddau to the east. They take their name from the twin peaks of Glyder Fach and Glyder Fawr, both of which are climbed on this walk. It is a magnificent, rugged and challenging walk amid superlative scenery – but it is also a strenuous walk suitable only for the fit and experienced mountain walker, as it involves some steep and energetic scrambling and difficult descents down scree and rock. It must be said too that this is definitely a walk for good summer weather, as even on a fine winter day snow and ice near the summits could make the going dangerous; it should be tackled only by walkers who are experienced in these conditions and properly equipped. But in the right conditions, when the views over the surrounding mountains are clear and extensive, this is a walk which will give tremendous exhilaration and satisfaction and will remain in the memory for a long while.

Start	Ogwen, at western end of Llyn Ogwen
Distance	5 miles (8 km)
Approximate time	6 hours
Parking	Car park at Ogwen by youth hostel. If full, plenty of parking areas about ¼ mile (0.5 km) to east along A5
Refreshments	Light refreshments at Ogwen
Ordnance Survey maps	Landranger 115 (Snowdon), Outdoor Leisure 17 (Snowdonia – Snowdon area)

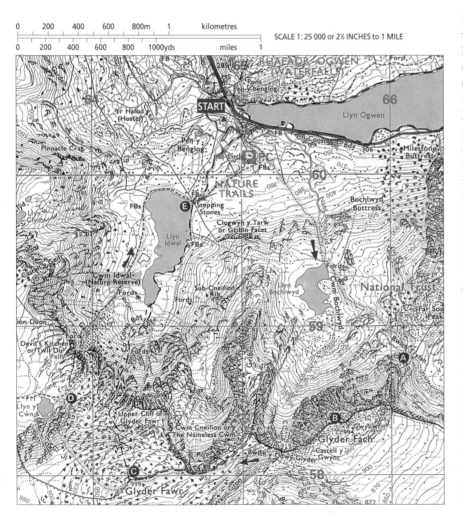

SCALE 1: 25 000 or 2½ INCHES to 1 MILE

Start by taking the uphill, stony path at the side of the car park, by the refreshment kiosk and toilet block. Climb a ladder-stile, cross a footbridge and continue, with excellent views of the Glyders in front and the distinctive bulk of Tryfan to the left. Where the main, well-constructed path bends to the right, keep ahead along a rather indistinct path making for Bochlwyd Falls in front. Climb fairly steeply to the right of the falls and at the top cross the stream on the left to continue along the left-hand side of Llyn Bochlwyd. Continue past the lake, climbing steadily to reach the col of Bwlch Tryfan and making for the ladder-stile ahead **A**.

From this col, which lies between Tryfan to the left and Glyder Fach to the right, there is a superb view looking back down to Llyn Bochlwyd and the whole length of the Nant Ffrancon Pass with the Menai Strait and Anglesey beyond. Climb the stile and turn right to begin the extremely steep and quite difficult ascent of Bristly Ridge, a daunting and formidable sight. There are two alternatives: either scramble up the rocks (if you like the challenge and have some experience – there are no exposed sections) or take the scree path to the left of the rock buttress. On reaching

the top continue across the rocks to a prominent pile of boulders – which includes the well-known overhanging 'cantilever' – and onto the weird-looking collection of rocks that constitute the summit of Glyder Fach at 3,262 feet (994 m) **B**. From here the views are breathtaking: a wide sweep takes in the Carneddau, Tryfan, Snowdon, the North Wales coast, Anglesey and Cardigan Bay, a superb panorama of the highest peaks south of the Scottish Highlands.

Continue to the next prominent group of rock pinnacles – Castell y Gwynt (the Castle of the Winds) – and either climb them or keep to the left of them. Descend and then climb again to rejoin the easy, gently ascending, cairned path to the summit of Glyder Fawr, with the impressive and familiar profile of Snowdon in the background all the while; the path keeps near the edge of the steep cliffs on the right to the summit, at 3,279 feet (999 m) **C**, another widely scattered collection of rocks from which there are magnificent views.

From here the descent begins and some care is required. Past the summit bear right to go down a steep, loose scree path to the small lake of Llyn y Cwn **D**. At the lake

Approaching the Glyders

Reaching the jagged pinnacles of Castell y Gwynt, having climbed to the summit of Glyder Fach and with Glyder Fawr ahead. Snowdon can be seen in the background

turn right across a boggy area to enter a broad shallow gully, after which there is a lengthy, rocky, steep climb down to Llyn Idwal, bearing left across the face of the cliff and descending by the right-hand side of the Devil's Kitchen. In Welsh this is appropriately called Twll Du (the Black Hole) as it is a dark, damp, deep, gloomy-looking cleft in the sheer rock face. In the latter stages of the descent a series of rocky steps helps the route down to the shores of Llyn Idwal.

The difficult and strenuous parts are now over and there is an easy, relaxing walk along the left-hand side of this beautiful lake, which is cradled by some of the most rugged and spectacular mountain terrain in Britain. Continue across the foot of the lake, cross a footbridge and turn left over a ladder-stile **Ⓔ** to follow a broad, rocky path. Bear left to rejoin the outward route and retrace your steps to the car park at Ogwen.

If you have any energy left, it is worth turning left for a few yards to see the impressive Ogwen Falls, where the river flows out of Llyn Ogwen to descend into the Nant Ffrancon valley.

Hartside, Salters Road and High Cantle

*This walk reveals one of the most enjoyable characteristics of the Cheviots –
their loneliness. For much of it you have to strain your eyes to see signs of
human occupation, if any are visible at all. Some of the way is on vague,
heathery tracks made either by sheep or shooting parties. It is wise to take a
compass and try the route only on a day of good visibility.*

Start	Hartside, 6 miles (9.5 km) west of A697, beyond Powburn and Ingram
Distance	8 miles (12.75 km)
Approximate time	4½ hours
Parking	On verge of public road before Hartside Farm
Refreshments	None
Ordnance Survey maps	Landranger 80 (Cheviot Hills & Kielder Forest), Pathfinder 487, NT 81/91 (Cheviot Hills, Central)

At Hartside take the farm road branching
to the left, which leads to Alnhammoor.
The River Breamish is soon on the right
forming a foreground for the lovely
Cheviot landscape. At Alnhammoor cross
the bridge, climb to the top of the incline

and turn left before the house on a path
waymarked as a permissive path. Turn
sharply to the right at the end of this short
path to pass behind the farmhouse **A**.

The Shank Burn is now on the left.
Keep to the lower path and cross the fence

at a stile bearing a footpath waymark just
beyond a stell (a round sheepfold). Cross a
streamlet, the Rowhope Burn, and follow
the path up through very tall bracken. At
this point frequent waymark posts show
the line of the path onto the open hillside.
However, sheep using them as scratching

posts sometimes uproot them from the
shallow soil, and they are not always
replaced with the arrows pointing in the
correct direction. If in doubt about the
path, climb gently in a south-westerly
direction across the heathery waste until
the view ahead opens up. Shank Burn

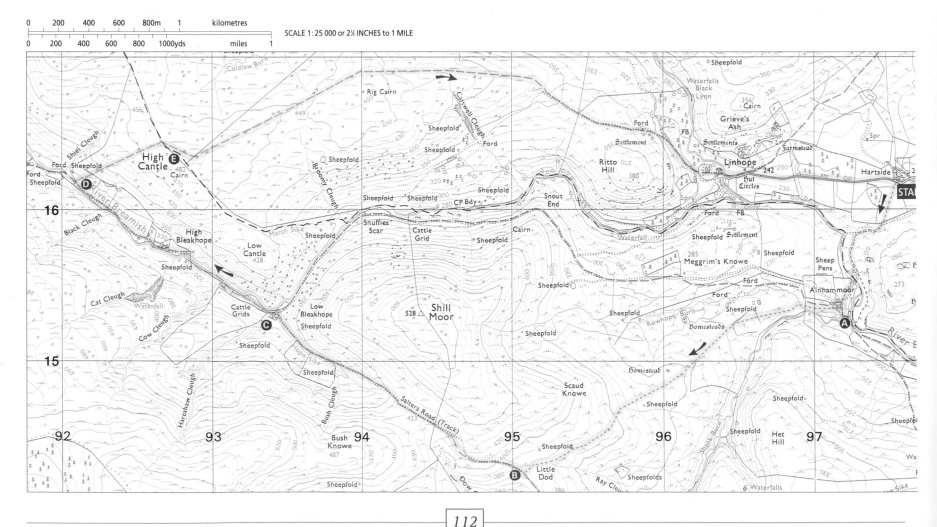

Today few people pass along Salter's Road below Shill Moor. Once it was a comparatively busy route with pack animals carrying salt from the coast

should still be on the left. Head for the dip between the low, rounded Little Dod on the left – with the cairn on the summit of Hogdon Law visible beyond – and the lower slopes of Shill Moor to the right.

When the view opens up even more the path continues heading south-westwards towards a black cattle-shelter, with a planting of pines on the saddle of Cushat Law beyond. It soon comes to the junction with Salters Road **B**; here the path carries straight on, in the direction shown by a blue bridleway waymark. The black cattle-shelter is now on the left.

Salters Road took its name from its regular use by salt traders who brought the precious commodity by this route from the salt-pans on the coast. Meat could only be

preserved in bygone days by smoking or salting, so salt was vital if folk were to have food other than grain in the winter. Salters Road was also busy with drovers and their flocks and herds, and the route was used too by whisky smugglers who carted the liquor from illicit stills hidden in remote valleys to customers in the lowland villages and towns.

The initial climb on the road is steepish but it soon levels out in a broad valley. After a gate the view westwards opens up with Bleakhope far below. The rough path follows the Hope Sike; there is quite a drop on the left but this is a very enjoyable part of the walk.

Anyone feeling fatigued at this point **C** could escape the rest of the walk by

returning to Alnhammoor by the bridleway which follows the valley of the Breamish River. But the walk continues by turning left at Low Bleakhope onto the farm road and following the stream upriver. Pass through a series of gates at High Bleakhope and follow the track past small areas of woodland. Quite often there is a heron fishing in the Breamish here.

After another, larger, clump of trees **D**, this time deciduous ones, climb up by the fence (taking care over wet ground) to a gate at the top. Keep on climbing to reach the top of High Cantle **E** where there is a mini-cairn and a stupendous view in every direction. Cross the fence so that the fence running north-east is on the left and head across the heather towards Rig Cairn

whose summit can be seen ahead below that of Great Standrop. There are twin rocky hummocks on the left, and no trace of the right of way on the ground. Take care here; it is no place to injure an ankle.

From Rig Cairn the view eastwards is revealed. Head in this direction, using paths made by the vehicles of shooting parties where possible. At first make for the plantation to the left of the conical Ritto Hill and then, when you can see it, for the gateway where three fences meet. Now follow a blue waymark which leads to a track going to Linhope Wood. A path to the left climbs to the waterfall – Linhope Spout – but the final part of our route bears right to reach Linhope itself, from where the road descends to Hartside.

Helvellyn

England's third highest mountain and one of Lakeland's most frequently climbed summits, Helvellyn offers a challenging and exciting fell walk and rewards the fit and energetic walker with a variety of terrain, dramatic scenery and distant views. After a lengthy, tiring climb along the edge of Grisedale, the final route to the summit is along the spectacular ridge of Striding Edge, followed by a rough scramble. The descent begins along the companion ridge of Swirral Edge before levelling off and dropping down. Although the edges are not as difficult as they appear from a distance, great care must be exercised on the traverse of both of them. Unless you are an experienced fell walker able to use a compass, this walk should definitely not be attempted in poor weather.

Start	Glenridding
Distance	8½ miles (13.5 km)
Approximate time	6 hours
Parking	Glenridding
Refreshments	Pubs and cafés in Glenridding
Ordnance Survey maps	Landranger 90 (Penrith, Keswick & Ambleside), Outdoor Leisure 5 (The English Lakes – North Eastern area)

Glenridding, once a lead-mining village, lies near the head of Ullswater, England's second longest lake, surrounded by high fells. As well as being a good centre for walking, a number of popular and scenic boat trips operate from the pier.

Start by walking along the main road towards Patterdale – a permissive path runs parallel to the road for much of the way. Just past the Patterdale sign cross Grisedale Bridge and turn right along a lane **A** which bears right, following the beck in its wooded valley below. At a public footpath sign turn right along a rough track **B**, cross the beck and keep ahead to a gate. Go through, continue to another gate, go through that and turn left along a path that climbs along the side of Grisedale, with excellent views towards the head of the dale framed by the peaks of St Sunday Crag and Dollywagon Pike.

A long, relentless climb of 1,500 feet (457 m) over 1½ miles (2.25 km) brings you to a stile in a wall known affectionately to walkers as the Hole in the Wall. Climb over and keep ahead, following a line of cairns through a wilderness of rocks to a large

pile of boulders called High Spying How. Negotiate these, keeping along the right-hand edge, and the 300-yard- (276 m) long Striding Edge is ahead. From a distance, or from photographs, Striding Edge looks positively hair-raising, giving the impression that you have to walk along a razor's edge of rocks. Although it is an exciting ridge walk which must be treated with respect, it is not as dangerous as it looks, except in high winds when it is definitely to be avoided. You are on it almost before you realise and there is a path a few yards below the ridge to the right. It is a tremendously exhilarating feeling to walk along it, with the crags on the right plunging down steeply to Red Tarn and the summit crest of Helvellyn just ahead. The most difficult section is scrambling over an awkward tower of rocks at the end.

Now comes the final haul to the summit (3,118 feet (949 m)) – some more steep, rough scrambling that brings you to the Gough memorial stone. This marks the

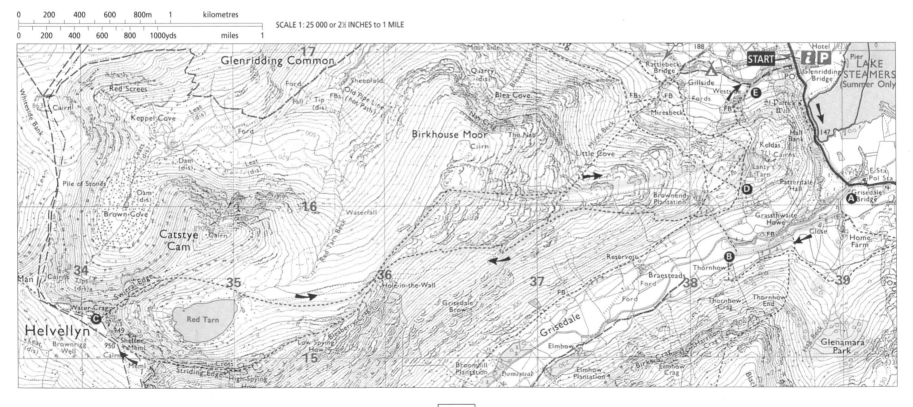

spot where the body of Charles Gough was discovered in 1803. He had been killed by a rock fall and when his skeletal remains were found three months later his dog was still guarding the body. After this sobering experience, it is but a short distance across the flat plateau to the summit wall **Ⓒ** from where in clear conditions there are incredible views over a large proportion of the Lake District, including Coniston Old Man, the Langdale Pikes, the Scafell range, Great Gable, High Street, Harter Fell, Gowbarrow Fell, the Derwent Fells, Blencathra and Skiddaw. Just to the south of the summit wall a stone commemorates the alleged first landing of an aeroplane on a British mountain, in 1926.

Keep ahead along the summit edge, and by a cairn turn sharp right to descend along Swirral Edge, which is similar to, though less awe-inspiring than, Striding Edge. Descend steeply with a fine view of Catstye Cam ahead, and after a while the path bears right, off the ridge, and drops down to the corner of Red Tarn. At this point there is a clear view of much of your recent route: Red Tarn lying in a natural amphitheatre with Striding Edge and Swirral Edge forming the two sides of it and pointing the way, like thin fingers, to the summit of Helvellyn. Cross a beck near the outlet from the tarn, bear slightly left and head across rough open country towards the line of crags on the right. There is no obvious path at this stage, but if you keep roughly parallel with, and just below, the line of crags, you pick up a path and after just over ½ mile (0.75 km) arrive at a ladder-stile about 100 yards (91 m) below the Hole in the Wall.

Do not climb the stile but turn left along a path that keeps by the wall on the right, heading downhill with views over Ullswater all the while. Near an outstanding viewpoint over Glenridding and Ullswater the path bears left away from the wall and heads down to a valley, but at this point keep straight ahead over the small hill in front and drop down to a ladder-stile by a wall corner. Climb over, turn right through

The walk along the ridge of Striding Edge below the summit of Helvellyn is one of the most exciting mountain experiences in Britain

a gate a few yards ahead, then turn left and continue down to the tree-encircled Lanty's Tarn, a lovely, quiet, half-hidden spot **Ⓓ**. Turn left at the tarn, go through a gate and make a brief detour to the right for one more minor ascent – to the top of Keldas. This is little more than a knoll but

from it there is a fine view down Ullswater – possibly the finest view of all, with the waters of the lake framed by pine trees. This is an ideal spot to relax before the final, short drop into Glenridding.

Return to the gate by the tarn and keep ahead along a broad, stony path which

heads downhill. On reaching a gate, do not go through it but turn sharp right down to another gate; go through and turn left through woodland to yet another gate. Go through that, turn right along a track **Ⓔ** and keep by the side of Glenridding Beck on the left back to the starting point. □

Ben Nevis

Ben Nevis, at 4,409 feet (1,344 m), is Britain's highest summit and as such has a special lure. Unfortunately many visitors with no real mountain experience casually decide to go and climb it, and every year there are casualties – and sometimes fatalities – as a result. Climbing Ben Nevis is a serious undertaking. The summit lies on the edge of the biggest cliffs of any British mountain, so navigation has to be confident and accurate. On a sunny day in Fort William the top of Ben Nevis can be in cloud or storm, and such weather can also sweep in far more quickly than an ascent can be made. The average mean temperature is just below freezing, and it can snow on any day of the year. On nine days out of ten the top stays in cloud. These are warning statistics. In winter the ascent should be tackled only by experienced mountaineers, able to navigate in blinding storms and technically skilled in using ice-axe and crampons. In any case, competent compass work is required.

Start	Glen Nevis youth hostel, visitor centre or Achintee
Distance	8 miles (12.75 km)
Approximate time	6–7 hours
Parking	Car parks at Glen Nevis youth hostel, visitor centre or Achintee
Refreshments	Pubs and cafés at Glen Nevis and Fort William
Ordnance Survey maps	Landranger 41 (Ben Nevis & Fort William), Outdoor Leisure 32 (Mountainmaster of Ben Nevis, The Grey Corries & The Mamores)

Boots are essential, and do carry plenty of spare clothing and plenty of refreshments. Take it slowly and steadily. You will be surprised how easy the climb proves: there is a path all the way! But alas, the path, even in summer, may be covered in snow on the summit plateau and navigation must be by map and compass if it is cloudy (footprints in the snow can be going anywhere). If you become at all worried, turn down while still able to do so. Don't hesitate to ask advice locally, in the youth hostel, camp site, Nevisport or tourist office. With experience, on a clear day, it is easy and marvellously satisfying.

The climb is a long, hard grind on rough and/or loose surfaces and snow lingers long on the summit plateau. Back down you will find it hard to believe that the Ben Nevis Race record time, for Fort William to the top and back, stands at under 1½ hours!

There are three regularly used starting points: the youth hostel in Glen Nevis or the nearby camp site – a footbridge from the hostel leads to a steep path up to join the Tourist Track; a car park at the visitor centre lower down the glen, where a footbridge crosses to a path which leads up to Achintee, the start of the Tourist Track;

and Achintee itself, where there is a bunkhouse and other accommodation (signposted, off the A82, on leaving Fort William). The second is the best starting point for the car-driver, as parking at the other places is limited.

From Achintee the Tourist Track climbs steadily up on a long, rising traverse. Originally built as a pony path for the Victorian summit observatory and hotel, the path is very stony and rough, but try to walk up slowly and steadily, and enjoy

pauses. Resist the temptation of 'short cuts'. Streams are all bridged. There are good views up the glen, and Stob Bàn looks impressive.

The path puts in a couple of elbow bends **A** and after these zigzags climbs at a steeper angle, from the Glen Nevis flank into the hollow of the Red Burn. When the back wall of this is reached the proper path elbows left **B** to turn up onto the broad saddle holding Lochan Meall an t-Suidhe (Half Way Loch). Don't take the worn short cut straight up the hillside.

There is a junction with a path bearing off left to traverse above the loch and down to the Alit a' Mhuilinn glen and the big Nevis cliffs, a route best left to the experts. The Tourist Track soon swings sharply right **C** and rises steadily up to the Red Burn **D**. An old pony shelter here was known as the Half Way Hut; with the more dangerous half lying ahead, this is the place to turn back if conditions or feelings are not encouraging. After this you are really committed to the grand adventure.

```
0    200  400  600  800m  1        kilometres
0    200  400  600  800  1000yds    miles    1
```

SCALE 1:27 778 or about 2¼ INCHES to 1 MILE

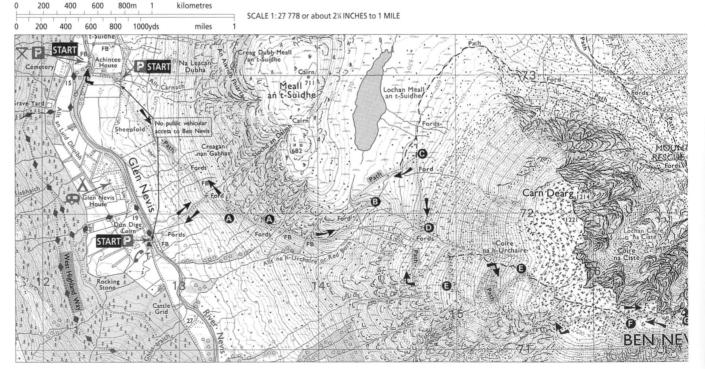

The awe-inspiring cliffs of Britain's highest mountain are a magnificent spectacle. Ben Nevis presents a challenge to walkers as well as climbers – but one which is not to be taken lightly

Ahead lies 1,000 feet (300 m) of stone and scree with the path gaining height in seemingly endless zigzags **E**. Keep to the path. When the angle relents you are on the summit plateau **F**, a huge, featureless area of boulders (or snow) at varying levels; tramp across this for ½ mile (0.75 km) to gain the summit. In places the path is very close to the cliffs, and if there is snow on the ground and bright mist the edge can be almost impossible to see.

There is no mistaking the summit **G**. There is a triangulation pillar on a cairn, the remains of the observatory buildings with a tiny emergency shelter on top, numerous unnecessary cairns, and a deal of litter. But what a place to be. Half of Scotland seems to be in view. There will almost certainly be other people about, so you can share the reward of being highest in Britain for a few moments.

Ben Nevis's real fame is as a climbers' mountain and as such it is world famous. A glance down the cliffs will demonstrate why. A vast array of precipices, ridges and gullies falls 2,000 feet (600 m) to the Allt a' Mhuilinn valley. The observatory operated from 1883 to 1904. There is no clear indication of the meaning of the name Nevis, which could have its roots in the Gaelic words for both heaven and hell.

The initial progress downwards may call for taking, and following, a careful compass bearing. The summit plateau can be a very confusing place and more people go astray leaving it for the descent than in any other way. The upward route is reversed in full, a three-hour descent for most, with care still needed at every step. There will be a grand feeling of achievement when the descent of Britain's highest mountain is completed. □

Useful organisations

**Association for the Protection
of Rural Scotland**
Gladstone's Land, 483 Lawnmarket,
Edinburgh EH1 2NT. Tel: 0131 225 7012

Cadw (Welsh Historic Monuments)
Brunel House, 2 Fitzalan Road, Cardiff CF2 1UY.
Tel: 01222 500200

Campaign for the Protection of Rural Wales
Tŷ Gwyn, 31 High Street, Welshpool,
Powys SY21 7JP. Tel: 01938 552525

Council for National Parks
246 Lavender Hill, London SW11 1LJ.
Tel: 0171 924 4077

Council for the Protection of Rural England
25 Buckingham Palace Road,
London SW1W 0PP.
Tel: 0171 976 6433

Countryside Commission
John Dower House, Crescent Place,
Cheltenham, Gloucestershire GL50 3RA.
Tel: 01242 521381

Countryside Council for Wales
Plas Penrhos, Ffordd Penrhos, Bangor,
Gwynedd LL5 72LQ. Tel: 01248 370444

English Heritage
23 Savile Row, London W1X 1AB.
Tel: 0171 973 3000

English Tourist Board
Thames Tower, Black's Road, Hammersmith,
London W6 9EL

Forestry Commission
Information Branch, 231 Corstorphine Road,
Edinburgh EH12 7AT.
Tel: 0131 334 0303

Historic Scotland
Longmore House, Salisbury Place,
Edinburgh EH9 1SH. Tel: 0131 244 3101

Long Distance Walkers' Association
7 Ford Drive, Yarnfield, Stone,
Staffordshire ST15 0RP

National Trust
36 Queen Anne's Gate, London SW1H 9AS.
Tel: 0171 222 9251

National Trust for Scotland
5 Charlotte Square, Edinburgh EH2 4DU.
Tel: 0131 226 5922

Ordnance Survey
Romsey Road, Maybush, Southampton
SO16 4GU. Tel: 01703 792912

Ramblers' Association
1/5 Wandsworth Road, London SW8 2BR.
Tel: 0171 582 6878

Scottish Natural Heritage
Information and Library Services,
2/5 Anderson Place, Edinburgh EH6 5NP.
Tel: 0131 554 9797

Scottish Rights of Way Society
John Cotton Business Centre, 10/2 Sunnyside,
Edinburgh EH7 5RA. Tel: 0131 652 2937

Scottish Tourist Board
23 Ravelston Terrace, Edinburgh EH4 3EU.
Tel: 0131 332 2433

Wales Tourist Board
Brunel House, 2 Fitzalan Road, Cardiff CF2 1UY.
Tel: 01222 499909

Youth Hostels Association
Trevelyan House, 8 St Stephen's Hill,
St Albans, Hertfordshire AL1 2DY.
Tel: 01727 855215

Ordnance Survey maps

Three series of Ordnance Survey maps together cover Britain at a scale which is ideal for exploring an area in detail, and especially for planning walks. All have maps at 1:25 000 scale (2½ inches to 1 mile or 4 cm to 1 km) and the maps covering England and Wales show rights of way which include the network of footpaths and bridleways which cross our countryside.

Outdoor Leisure maps cover most of Britain's national parks and a number of popular areas of outstanding natural beauty. The size of the area covered varies across the

series. **Explorer maps** cover Britain's well-known but less-explored recreational areas and beauty spots. The size of the area covered varies from 12 miles (20 km) square to 19 miles by 14 miles (30 km by 22 km). **Pathfinder maps** complete the coverage of Britain at this scale. Most Pathfinder maps cover an area 12 miles (20 km) by 6 miles (10 km). Packed with detail, the maps in all three series are invaluable for tourists and holidaymakers as well as walkers and climbers. Tourist information includes youth hostels, camping and caravan sites, picnic areas and viewpoints.

A series of all-purpose maps at 1:50 000 scale (1¼ inches to 1 mile or 2 cm to 1 km) also covers Britain. The 204 **Landranger maps** are full of information to help you get to know an area and are ideal for helping to find the start of individual Pathfinder walks. Each covers an area 25 miles (40 km) square and like other Ordnance Survey maps has National Grid numbers so that any feature can be given a unique reference number. Tourist information such as camping and caravan sites, picnic areas and viewpoints is given, and rights of way information such as footpaths and

bridleways is also shown on Landranger maps covering England and Wales.

Travelmaster maps are motorists' route-planning maps which cover Britain in nine sheets. The first sheet is the overall Great Britain Routeplanner at 1:625 000 scale (1 inch to 10 miles or 1 cm to 6.25 km), and the other eight sheets are at 1:250 000 scale (1 inch to 4 miles or 1 cm to 2.5 km). They are an ideal guide to the location of individual Pathfinder walks. Selected tourist information is shown, and the distance between towns, and a separate place names index is included.

Pathfinder Guides

The Pathfinder Guide series of walking guides to different regions of Britain covers most of England and Wales and large parts of Scotland. These practical guides are designed to take on walks and fit easily into pocket or rucksack.

Each one has twenty-eight walks which are described in detail and have the routes marked on extracts from Ordnance Survey Pathfinder or Outdoor Leisure maps.

The walks, which range from easy half-day family strolls to longer and more demanding

day walks for more experienced ramblers, are colour coded according to the level of difficulty. As well as easy-to-follow route directions, details are given of interesting features en route, colour photographs show the scenery, general descriptions outline the

nature of each walk and information is given about parking, where to eat and drink and the relevant Ordnance Survey maps.

In addition the guides have introductions to the regions and addresses of useful local organisations.

Titles in the series
(Walks from them are on the following pages in this book)

Brecon Beacons and Glamorgan Walks
  (92, 102)
Chilterns and Thames Valley Walks
  (22, 34, 62)
Cornwall Walks (70)

Cotswold Walks (90)
Dartmoor Walks (20)
Dorset Walks (56, 96)
Edinburgh and the Borders Walks
Exmoor and the Quantocks Walks (64)
Fort William and Glen Coe Walks (30, 116)
Hampshire Walks (36)
Heart of England Walks (24, 38, 86)
Isle of Wight Walks (44)

Kent Walks (50)
Lake District Walks (52, 84, 114)
Lancashire and Cheshire Walks
Loch Lomond and Trossachs Walks (46)
Mid Wales and the Marches Walks
More Lake District Walks
Norfolk and Suffolk Walks (48, 78, 104)
Northumbria Walks (60, 80, 98, 112)
North York Moors Walks (58, 74)

Peak District Walks (18)
Pembrokeshire and Gower Walks (72)
Perthshire Walks (88)
Snowdonia, Anglesey and the Lleyn
  Peninsula Walks (110)
Surrey and Sussex Walks (40, 66, 76)
Wye Valley and Forest of Dean Walks
  (16, 32, 100)
Yorkshire Dales Walks (26, 106)

Index

Acknowledgements

The publishers would like to thank the staff of the national park authorities, county councils, tourist information centres, National Trust offices and the Forestry Commission, and many others who have given much valuable advice and assistance, including members of the Ramblers' Association who rewalked many of the routes chosen for this book.

Authors of the Pathfinder Guides from which the walks in this book were taken are:
John Brooks, Hamish Brown, Brian Conduit, Anne-Marie Edwards, Jenny Plucknett and John Watney.

Flora and fauna text: Reg Jones
Flora and fauna illustrations: Michael Rowe
Other illustrations: Don Fisher

Picture credits
Hamish Brown pp. 30, 31, 117; Brian Conduit p. 111; Mike Edwards pp. 37, 44, 45;
John Watney pp. 88, 89.
Other pictures © Jarrold Publishing.